Rambunctious
Reflections

The rollicking memoirs of an English Boy in Kenya

Leonard J. Gill

National Library of Canada Cataloguing in Publication

Gill, Leonard J., 1930-
    Rambunctious reflections / Leonard J. Gill.
Includes bibliographical references.
ISBN 1-55395-107-7
    1. Gill, Leonard J., 1930- --Childhood and youth. 2. Kenya--Biography. I. Title.

DT433.576.G54A3 2002   967.62'03'092   C2002-904435-9

TRAFFORD

This book was published *on-demand* in cooperation with Trafford Publishing.
On-demand publishing is a unique process and service of making a book available for retail sale to the public taking advantage of on-demand manufacturing and Internet marketing.
On-demand publishing includes promotions, retail sales, manufacturing, order fulfilment, accounting and collecting royalties on behalf of the author.

Suite 6E, 2333 Government St., Victoria, B.C. V8T 4P4, CANADA

Phone	250-383-6864	Toll-free	1-888-232-4444 (Canada & US)
Fax	250-383-6804	E-mail	sales@trafford.com
Web site	www.trafford.com	TRAFFORD PUBLISHING IS A DIVISION OF TRAFFORD HOLDINGS LTD.
Trafford Catalogue #02-0821		www.trafford.com/robots/02-0821.html

10   9   8   7   6   5   4   3

Acknowledgments

My deepest appreciation goes to the members of the Glenwood Springs Writer's Workshop, without whom this book would never have seen the light of day.

The gentle yet professional critiques of Karen Chamberlain, Carol Bell, Pat Conway, Kristin Carlson, Philip Wheelock, Valerie Haugen, Taylor Liebmann, to mention just a few, have been essential and encouraging. I have been fortunate to find such erudite and accomplished advisors so close to home.

Last but certainly not least, I thank artist, Jack Niswanger for his humorous cartoons which add so much to the narrative.

Dedication

Without Kaye, this book would be merely a smile on my face as I reminisce. My dear wife, Kaye, has been patiently inspiring, encouraging and goading. She helps me with American English usage and spelling. She tells me when I'm wrong. She's always right. She shows me how to operate the word processor, the printer and how and when to replace passages so that the book flows easily.

Rambunctious Reflections

Table of Contents

Prologue

Page #

1   Brief geography of Kenya.   Mt. Kilimanjaro.

2   Borders cut through tribal areas. Post independence return of tribal wars. World's media silence on the return of tribalism.

3   AIDS.

3   Rain seasons.

4   **East Africa discovered.** 1850 on, explorers, missionaries and hunters.

         Earlier visitors - Phoenicians, Vasco da Gama. The natives. Decimation by famine and disease.

5   **Slavery in East Africa.**

6   Slavery continues today.

7   **Map of Kenya.**

Chapter 1

1   Joan Woods

6   Mum produces a problem.

Chapter 2

8   My family history in Africa.

9   Dad's war.

10   WW1 ends…

12   Life at Magadi.

13   Grab a spouse.

13   Disciplinary action. An old soldier disappears.

15   Honeymoon.

Chapter 3
19   Prince of Wales
23   PoW visits the Delamere farm.
25   To hunt or to....
26   Beryl and the coupe d'etat.

Chapter 4
27   A right Charlie, or The Great White Hunter.

Chapter 5
38   A Quiet American.
41   Misidentification.
42   Myrtle and the big gray thing.

Chapter 6
45   Doc Forbes's bedside manner.
47   Just too isolated.
47   Sudden death in a whirlwind.
48   Near misses.
49   Nairobi via Carshalton Beeches.
51   A bit too much warmth.
51   Sister Elizabeth.
52   The Passion Wagon.
54   Matthew's lion.
55   The Key.
56   A bloody WHAT????
57   Father Christmas and the Ghillie-ghillie man.

Chapter 7
59   Growing up.
59   Greater affluence and more servants.
60   Sewing machine repairman and Ovaltine.
61   Clever lad - lessons learned.
62   Crime and Punishment.
64   My new territory.
64   Meet my new pal.

Chapter 8
68   An intrusion - Margaret.
70   Formal education is on the horizon.
72   Miss Thomas.
76   On to Muthaiga School.

Chapter 9
82   Mum doesn't learn to play golf.
85   Mum, the Firefighter.

Chapter 10
86   A succession of schools.
87   St. Andrews School.
88   Scientific experiments.
91   Kenton College.
92   Hey, Mr Hitler
94   Blevets.
97   The Enemy at Our Door?
99   Military discipline.

Chapter 11
103   Solus

Chapter 12
108   Public = Privately Owned. Government = Publicly Owned.
109   An indifferent scholar at Kenton.
111   A gentleman's club?

Chapter 13
115   Artful boxing.
117   An eerie experience.
118   And he's a friend?
119   'Bosom' Martin and I break records.

Prologue

I was born in Kenya in December, 1930, when the country was a British colony. Kenya is in eastern Africa with the Equator running across the middle. The Great Rift Valley runs, some say, from the Dead Sea, southward through the Gulf of Aqabah, it follows the Red Sea southwards, and then veers south westward through Djibouti, then south through Ethiopia, through western Kenya and on southwards through Tanzania, to Malawi. An off-shoot curls westwards south of Lake Victoria and then north through a series of lakes - Tanganyika, Kivu, Rutangze to Lake Albert. Parts of the route taken by the Great Rift Valley are well defined, while in other sections it almost peters out. But it can be followed, easily enough, for most of its course. In Kenya there are several lakes in the Valley. These are soda lakes with a high chemical content. The Valley has had a significant effect, over a considerable period, on Kenya's climate and, hence, its flora, fauna and human population. Kenya for the most part, has a wonderful climate, as the land rises quickly from the coast and the altitude reduces what might otherwise be enervating temperatures. Nairobi, the capital, is at an altitude of almost 6,000 feet above sea level, and lies a mere seventy miles or so south of the Equator. Mount Kenya - altitude over 17,000 ft. - is on the Equator. Its peaks are permanently snow covered. Mount Kilimanjaro - altitude a little over 19,000 ft - lies about 200 miles south of the Equator, just south of Tanzania's northern border. The top of this upturned pudding-bowl-shaped mountain is also permanently snow covered. Mount Kilimanjaro was, at one time, in British East Africa, now Kenya. It was given by Queen Victoria to her kinsman, the German Kaiser, as a birthday present.

This act epitomizes the attitudes, at the time, of the colonial powers towards Africa. In many parts, borders between areas of influence, now countries, cut through tribal

1

areas. Thus, Masailand is divided by the border between Kenya and Tanzania. In the north east, Kenya's border with Somalia cuts through land occupied by Somali people, so that some of them are now Kenyans, while the bulk of their kinsfolk are considered as citizens of Somalia. How these anomalies will be eventually ironed out is a moot point. Perhaps it will necessitate the complete fragmentation of Africa, and re-coalescence into more natural demographic areas. Or will federations, uniting groups of like countries, dilute border problems?

At present we see a great deal of terrible ethnic genocide and tribal conflict, some of which has been going on ever since African countries gained independence 40 years ago. On the other hand, it is noted that confederations have failed. Examples include the Central African Federation that comprised Northern and Southern Rhodesia and Nyasaland, now Zambia, Zimbabwe and Malawi, and the East African Community which comprised Kenya, Uganda and Tanzania. Tribalism, largely quiescent during colonial times, has erupted again, costing the lives of millions throughout Africa. The hero of South Africa, Nelson Mandela, had no sooner become South Africa's world media-acknowledged leader, than tribal killing re-commenced. The bodies of tribesmen were to be seen being washed down rivers as killings broke out.

The world media has been silent on this turn of events. Is the media morally and ethically sick? Why have so many whites, born and bred in Africa, left the land they loved, and the people they wanted to see happy, free and successful? The return of tribalism, corruption, rife at all levels of society, and a total lack of moral fibre amongst some new leaders has led to ethical degeneration and moral turpitude. The world's media remains silent, and shrugs off any responsibility to disseminate the truth. The criticism of administrations, that was deemed a worthy cause in colonial times, and prior to 'democracy' in South Africa, is no longer a media issue.

AIDS is sweeping through Africa and there seems to be little that can be done to stop the spread of this frightful disease. Whole villages have been wiped out along the main road routes used by drivers of heavy trucks, who are believed to be one cause of the spread of the disease. A change in the attitude of the people towards promiscuity is vital, but, since the disease doesn't initially cause visible symptoms, many Africans do not believe that sex is the cause of the problem. Prevalent opinions lead Africans to ask, "Haven't the doctors of the Western World a cure for AIDS? Doesn't a jab of some wonder anti-biotic do the job? Is the Western World deliberately denying Africans a cure, so that Africa will become depopulated and re-colonization can take place?"

The Western World claimed that AIDS started in Africa. This was politically unacceptable in Africa. On the other hand, many Africans point out, prostitution, sodomy and blood transfusions are Western practices. Only in the large, cosmopolitan cities of Africa are such practices prevalent, brought to Africa by Westerners. Aren't they the origin and the cause of the spread of the disease? These beliefs and questions have to be understood, and the necessary education introduced.

Kenya has two rainy seasons, one in April, when very heavy rain can be expected after a dry hot period. The 'short rains', or 'grass rains', occur in November, and are only sufficient to get the grass to turn green again. There is a cool, cloudy spell from July through September. The hottest period is from December through to April when the 'long rains' start. By that time the country is very dry and dead grass crunches underfoot. Clouds build up over a period of days and then weeks. They become darker and darker until they are an ominous black. There is little breeze, and the heat is oppressive.

Then, one day big rain drops fall. They auger a storm. But, after a few minutes, they stop, and disappointment leads to frustration, short tempers and even suicides. Two or three days later, a strong wind heralds a further fall of big

3

drops. And then the storm breaks. It rains. And how it rains. Within minutes the temperature drops, and the dust is washed off the grass and leaves. In minutes there is evidence of green foliage where there had been nothing but dry, dusty, dead leaves. Nervous tension is dissipated. People smile again, and even small boys are hugged by their parents.

East Africa Discovered

During the 1850s to the 1870s explorers, missionaries and big game hunters started to take an interest in East Africa. Men like David Livingstone, Sir Henry Morton Stanley, Sir Richard Burton, John Hanning Speke, Joseph Thomson and others were to inspire further exploration and hunting expeditions.

There had been earlier visitors from distant countries, including the Phoenicians but, apart from the Arabs from what is now the Saudi Arabian peninsula and Syria, the foreigners had moved on and had never penetrated the hinterland. Vasco da Gama, the Portuguese navigator, who had discovered the sea route to India in 1498 by way of the Cape of Good Hope, visited East Africa, and left evidence of his visit in navigational aids erected at Malindi. These aids were in the form of two monoliths, one near the shore, and the other a few yards inland. When lined up, one behind the other, by a ship at sea, they indicated the safe route through the reef into Malindi bay. He also had erected a stone beacon on a point stretching some distance out to sea. There are also the ruins of a church he had built.

When the explorers, missionaries and hunters arrived in Kenya in the 1850s, they found a land with some forty-five tribes, each with their own language. They had no written history, and were considered to be primitive people. Vast areas were uninhabited or sparsely inhabited. This situation was later claimed by African politicians to be the result of famine due to a series of droughts, tribal warfare and disease,

4

including rinderpest and anthrax, diseases that affect ruminants including cattle, and spread by buffalo. Since there was no written history, claims by politicians could not be proven. Each tribe, they asserted, had been forced to shrink back into their ethnic territory. The written diaries of the European explorers and hunters contradicted the politicians' claims.

From the turn of the 20th century, settlers had begun to arrive as a result of the British Government's advertising campaign aimed at the British elite, who were lured by the possibilities of inexpensive land, big game hunting and an idyllic climate. The uninhabited areas were to be known as the White Highlands, and were considered to be suitable for European settlement. The British Government delineated the White Highlands and other areas as Government land, as well as tribal areas or Reserves. This was to ensure that further tribal warfare and encroachment of tribal areas by land-hungry settlers or tribal neighbors, was more easily detected and controlled.

Slavery in East Africa

The Arabs from Syria and Oman had been operating a slave trade for some 800 years with the help of local Africans, who rounded up men from other tribes, and brought them to the coast. The Arabs had set up a Sultanate on the island of Zanzibar, off the coast of what is now Tanzania, from where they could conduct their trade in safety. The British ended this slave trade in the 1830s. A war in 1890 against the new Sultan of Zanzibar, who had usurped power with the aim of reintroducing the slave trade, that lasted less than 40 minutes - the shortest war in history - in which shells from British warships were fired at the Island, ended his aspiration. Anglican missionaries then began a study of the *lingua franca* Kiswahili. A dictionary of the language was completed in 1903.

It is reported that a slave trade continues today with over thirty thousand African slaves in the hands of Muslims in northern Sudan and across North Africa. How is it possible to reconcile the constant, frenetic criticism of the Slave Trade between West Africa and North America and the Caribbean, which ended in the mid 1800s, with the total omission of any criticism of the slave trade conducted by Arabs, which went on for so many hundreds of years, and is continued today? And, is it not extraordinary that some African-Americans adopt Arab names?

It is not, perhaps, generally known that one of the first slave trade connections with Africa was the settlement of European slaves in the Cape of Good Hope in the early sixteenth century. They were required to provision visiting ships with fresh meat, fruit and vegetables in return for an increased measure of freedom.

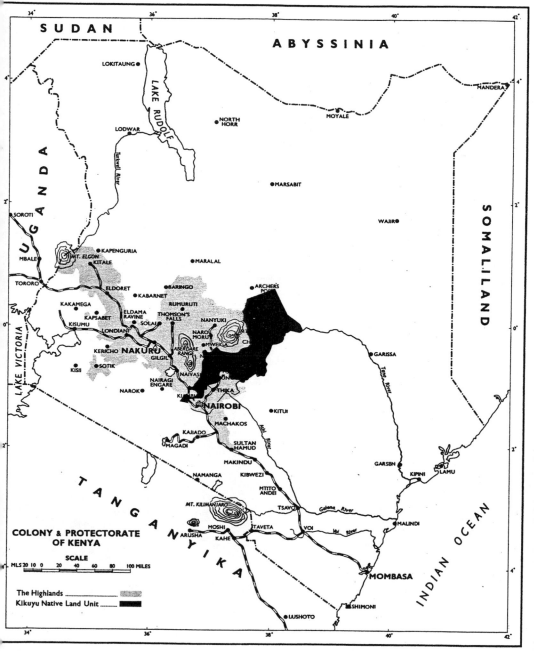

COLONY & PROTECTORATE
OF KENYA

SCALE

MLS 20 10 0   20   40   60   80   100 MILES

The Highlands ....
Kikuyu Native Land Unit ....

1895 - 1963

1

The Lovely Joan Woods and the Magical Medicine Man

WAAAAHHHH! All of Nairobi heard my strident scream of pain and terror. A large piece of glass had cut into my right arm and stuck there. Blood was everywhere. Joan looked impatiently at me, clearly wishing I wasn't a clumsy, awkward, stupid boy who had come to spoil her day.

Joan Woods was my first love. I was a little over four years old when arrangements were made for me to spend a few hours at her home. She was six months my senior, and a domineering female. Mum wanted to go shopping, and didn't want to leave me at home on my own, where I might set fire to the house, abuse the servants or put snails in my sister, Elizabeth's, bed, and she certainly didn't want to take me with her into the shops where I might purloin valuable stock by artful shoplifting. So, arrangements were made for me to spend the day with Joan Woods. The appointment would take me away from my dog, Joe, for a few hours, but I was eager to display my charms to any girl who was not my sister.

Passion welled up in me, and if Joan was to turn out to be indifferent, I had enough ardor for both of us. I discussed the forthcoming event with Joe. He had little to say, appeared bored, and dozed off to sleep at my feet. Mum made sure I was dressed to impress. I had to don a clean white shirt, clean blue shorts, clean knee length gray stockings, polished black shoes and a pith helmet.

"If you get your clothes dirty, I'll kill you," threatened my loving Mum.

Imagine my disappointment when I met Joan wearing dirty dungarees, worn out sneakers and a straw hat, part of which had apparently been a donkey's breakfast. In retaliation I discontinued pulling up my stockings which were inclined to comply with gravity and work their way down to my ankles, concertina style.

Mrs. Woods, I'm sure, had let my parents assume she would be staying at her house to keep an eye on us. But Mrs Woods had to go shopping, and Joan and I were left in the care of the Woods' servants.

Joan wanted to build two inch wide cement roads for her toy cars. I was to do the fetching and carrying while she did the civil engineering. There was a bag of cement in Mr. Woods' garage, sand in a heap and a stand pipe for water in the garden. I was issued with a glass bottle to bring water from the stand pipe, and I had to be on my toes to fetch whatever Joan needed quickly, as cement mixing is a demanding activity.

It was when I was racing back from filling the bottle that I tripped and fell. The bottle smashed, and I fell onto it. So I screamed - just to get a bit of sympathy, you understand. The house-boy ran out of the house, took me to the stand pipe, and held my arm under the running faucet. The shard of glass sticking out of my arm did look rather unpleasant, so I continued screaming.

A passing Masai tribesman came into the garden to see what the fuss was about.

"*Shauri gani? Kwa sababu mtoto nalia?*" ("What's the problem? Why is the child crying?") he asked.

"*Anaumiwa*", ("He is injured"), replied the servant.

2

"Wapi?" ("Where?") asked the Masai.

"Mkononi" ("On the arm"). The servant showed the tribesman the wound.

"Aaah, *pole* (pronounced poleh) *mtoto*", (freely translated: "Oh, take it easy young'un"). The Masai was trying to soothe a frightened four-year-old.

He took one look, deftly removed the shard, instructed the servant to get a bandage, and then set off searching around the garden. I was impressed by the tall, lean warrior who was wearing, over one shoulder, a red blanket belted about his waist. As he moved, the blanket parted to reveal an eighteen inch long scabbard from which protruded the handle of a *sime* (pronounced seemeh), the traditional short, double-edged sword of the Masai. He walked with an elegant grace, and somewhat overwhelmed by his commanding figure, I trailed after him, hurrying to keep up. He found a safari of ants, and taking one of the big soldier ants, held it so that its large mandibles bridged the wound. He held the lips of the wound together as the ant closed its jaws across it. When it was firmly attached, the Masai nipped off its body with his thumb nail, leaving the head with its jaws imbedded firmly on either side of the wound. I was so startled and amazed at the tribesman's competence, and obvious confidence, that I quit screaming.

My new-found Masai friend repeated the suturing with one soldier ant after another, until the wound was completely closed. He then took me back to the stand pipe where he washed my arm again. Leaving me with my arm under a stream of water, he went to find a large leaf which he placed over the wound, and bound it on with the bandage the servant had brought. I thanked him by putting my left palm on the inside of my right elbow, extending my right hand in the gesture of thanks that I had learned. He took my hand momentarily, smiled and strode away. (Years later I was told that to say *Asante* (Thanks) may be taken as a sarcastic expression used by someone who considers a reward too meager. I had unconsciously used the acceptable gesture that I had observed Africans use.)

Dad came to collect me at lunch time, and was told the story of what had happened by the servant. He took me home, and told Mum not to remove the bandage, saying that the tribesman had almost certainly known what he was about. Each soldier ant would have injected a mild acid as it closed its jaws, and this would act as a disinfectant. The leaf too would have been specially selected for its medicinal properties. So the bandage was left on for about ten days, and when it was removed, the wound had healed and the ants' heads had become detached. A scar, over sixty-seven years later, is still faintly visible.

Sadly, that was the end of my romance. Mrs. Woods was judged to have been too casual in leaving Joan at the mercy of me, the local roué, who had probably stage-managed the bloody incident in an attempt to impress the unchaperoned Joan. I consoled myself with the thoughts that Joan had been bossy, and had made no effort to entertain or amuse me. We hadn't entered into any intellectual discussions, nor had we searched for wolf spiders' holes in the ground to tempt them out so that we could catch them and make them fight to see whose was the best combatant. Such pastimes are eagerly entered into by small boys in Kenya. Joan should have known. Nor had she made any effort to dress in her best party-frock for the occasion. She had shown a high degree of disregard for me, not even coming to my aid when I was wailing for sympathy. The wretched wench was not worth worrying about. My romantic aspirations relapsed and went onto the back burner.

I was happy that Mum didn't keep her promise to kill me if I dirtied my clothes. They were covered, not only with mud but also blood, and this may have turned her wrath to sympathy. I talked the whole affair over with Joe. He wagged his stumpy tail, welcoming my attention, but soon became bored with my story, and dozed off to sleep at my feet.

Mum Produces a Problem.

Mum hadn't wanted a son and it was agreed that, if one came along, it would be Dad's responsibility to bring him up. The problem was that Dad was fifteen years older than Mum and was forty-one years of age when I came into the world. Not only had he never had much to do with children until my Mum produced my elder sister, Elizabeth, he was conscientious and worked long hours.

So, Mum had to shoulder the responsibility, and though she showed little reluctance, it was not a job she relished nor one in which she felt confident. And I didn't help. I was idle, slow to learn, unjustifiably over-confident, feckless and reckless, so Mum had a thankless job to do. But a leopard cannot change his spots. I am me and no matter how my parents tried, my spots were firmly attached. So my parents had to accept Leonard, spots and all. Once they accepted this, we got along much better.

Mum had shed tears over me a short time after my birth. The hospital in which I was born had green wooden window shutters, which opened outwards. The steel window casements opened into the rooms - a daft arrangement I suggest. After my birth, I was cleaned, polished and wrapped up for presentation to my disappointed mother who, after a short while, asked the nurse to dispose of me somewhere. The nurse thought my mother was joking, and put me in a cradle under the open window. She bent low over the cot and cooed as women do, and as she stood up, nurse banged her head on the sharp corner of the steel window frame.

Poor Mum, drained by giving birth to a XXL sized baby, and then learning that the wretched thing was male, burst into tears. She realized that life was never to be the way she had dreamed. The whole thing was just too devastating, and her sobs evinced her recognition of her plight. Both the injured nurse and I survived, unaware of the havoc my arrival had caused. Had I known how Mum was reacting to my advent, I might have turned round and gone back to whence I had come. But I was ignorant, and didn't even show any concern for the injured nurse.

My attitude was to typify the 'I'm all right, Jack' opinions I was to adopt, along with the other leopard spots that brought pain to my parents, disdain from my sisters, and little respect from anyone else.

2

My family history in Africa

Both my parents were English, my father, Harold Warren Gill, from Kent, and my mother, Mary, but called Molly, from Northumberland.

Dad left England for South Africa in 1912 after gaining a science degree and a post-graduate qualification from London University. He secured a position as a lecturer at Cape Town University, after being hastily granted an honorary degree to circumvent the South African government's requirement that all university lecturers hold South African university degrees.

Having landed the job, Dad let the press know how the university authorities were dodging the government's policy. This caused both embarrassment for the university, and Dad's departure from Cape Town. But he quickly succeeded in landing a job as lecturer with the Johannesburg School of Mines. His qualifications in industrial chemistry were sorely needed in South Africa at the time.

Dad's war

The outbreak of the World War in 1914 resulted in Dad's joining the British Light Artillery to fight in what was then German South-West Africa - now Namibia. Dad claimed that his war experience in GSWA merely covered a march from Cape Town to Walvis Bay, some 800 miles up the south-west coast of Africa, and back. But there was more to it than that.

One of his comrades was an African-American actor, who had volunteered to serve with the British forces in South Africa. He must have been a remarkable character. He certainly made a lasting impression on my Dad. The area in which they were serving is a desert, and can become very cold at night. One freezing night, this black man covered a wounded British soldier with his greatcoat, an act which none of the white soldiers had thought to do. I do not know the name of this good Samaritan, so I'll call him Ed.

Ed called my Dad Hal (a name that stuck for the rest of his life) instead of Harold, taught him how to tie a bow tie, and advised him never to have anything to do with thespians. How an African American actor happened to be serving in the British Light Artillery in German South West Africa in 1914 in the Kaiser War, must be a story of its own. Unfortunately, Dad never elaborated on this tale, but did have one rather serious anecdote to recount.

Dad's unit had captured a German base, and Dad had relieved the Germans of a book of recipes on the making of booze. Dad's university studies had included learning technical German, so he recognized the book for what it was. In no time the Hooch Book enabled Dad, aided by Ed, to make spirituous liquors that were very eagerly sought after by all the soldiers in the unit. Dad's popularity rose, and so did Ed's.

I have no doubt that they were excused from many chores, so that booze production could proceed without unnecessary interruption. Unfortunately, Dad was still called upon to fight, and during one skirmish he was wounded. As he was being removed from the battlefield on a stretcher, Ed was in attendance, and Dad instructed him that, in no circumstances, was he to attempt to make any booze. Not only was Ed unable to read the Hooch Book, he was also ignorant of some of the procedures and tests, so there was a danger that poisonous booze might be made.

Unfortunately, while Dad was in the hospital, Ed was persuaded to make a batch. I have little doubt that his life would have been in jeopardy had he refused to comply with market demands. The result of this was that eleven soldiers died. Ed was sent back to civilian life. This happened swiftly and quietly while Dad was still recuperating from his injury. Ed disappeared into oblivion without leaving a forwarding address.

WWI ends

The war in GSWA ended, and Dad was sent up to fire shells at the enemy in German East Africa - subsequently Tanganyika, now Tanzania. He arrived there in 1917, and the German forces were finally persuaded to lay down their arms in 1919, some six months after the War had ended in Europe. The remarkable German General, Count von Letto Vorbek, had refused to believe the Kaiser had agreed to the signing of the Armistice until no further ammunition arrived for the German troops, confirming the rumor that the War was over.

The Brits had built a single track railway in British East Africa - subsequently Kenya - from Kilindini Harbour, Mombasa, across the country to Port Florence on Lake Victoria. This railway had been started in 1900 and was completed in 1903. Parliament in London had been led to believe that this would be an economically viable proposition once British settlers started to export agricultural produce.

After World War I, advertisements appeared in British journals encouraging the aristocracy and professionals to settle in Kenya Colony. The ads said there was plenty of sun, hunting, shooting and fishing. This was to attract the leisure classes to leave cold, windy, war-weary Britain, where it had become quite difficult to find 'decent domestic staff'. Another enticement was the possibility of finding willing natives that the Memsahib could train to be house servants - while the Bwana went about the place farming, hunting, fishing and that sort of thing. The settlers would need the services of doctors, dentists, pharmacists, and possibly parsons, and together all the settlers would provide the railway with business, and make it profitable.

Settlers had arrived before WW I, but not in sufficient numbers so, at the end of the war in East Africa, British soldiers who had served there were offered land. The idea was that they would farm large parcels of land efficiently, and would provide surpluses of agricultural produce for export. The farmers would have to import goods, hopefully of British manufacture. In this way the railway would be put to use and would become commercially viable.

Later, starting from the 1920s, Kenya's agricultural industry was to become the major export earner. European farmers in Kenya overcame the diseases affecting crops and livestock that they hadn't experienced in Europe. They also believed that if their produce was of very high quality, it would sell at high prices on the export market. Many of Kenya's agricultural products were of high quality. Coffee, tea, dairy products, pig products and others were produced in small quantities compared with the world's largest producers, but the prices for Kenya's export produce were among the highest.

Dad had applied for, and was granted 400 acres of land in what is now Kenya's best tea country. But, at the time the property was isolated being seventy miles from the nearest railway station. In addition, Dad was not a farmer. So he sold his farm for what amounted to the average monthly salary for a European, and got a job as Assistant Chemist at Lake Magadi. His boss was the Chief Chemist, John Chambers, an industrial chemist in his mid-forties. Lake Magadi is some sixty miles from Nairobi and, at that time, could be reached only by freight train or by walking. But at least the job was one he was qualified to do.

Life at Magadi

Lake Magadi is a shallow soda lake and the pinkish soda ash, used in glass and soap manufacture, has been collected and processed since 1909. The Magadi Soda Company was originally owned by the Brunner Monde group, which was to be taken over, in the mid-twenties, by Imperial Chemical Industries (ICI), one of Britain's biggest industrial corporations. Dad was promoted to Chief Chemist when John Chambers was posted back to civilization in Mombasa, to become manager of the company's port facility at Kilindini.

John Chambers had gone out to Kenya in 1909 to work for the Magadi Soda Company, leaving his family in England, since Magadi, being isolated, had no facilities for families. The only way to get to Magadi was by freight train on a spur line from Kajiado, a station on the main line from Mombasa to Nairobi. In those days white settlers were offered four year contracts, which provided a six month holiday in Britain after three and a half years of service in Kenya. Thus, John Chambers returned to his family in Monkseton, near Newcastle, every three-and-a-half years. The eldest daughter, Mary but called Molly, later to become my mother, had been born in 1905. She was followed by two more daughters, Norah and Ada, and then in 1917 a son, John, called Jack. Not surprisingly, perhaps, they were born at four year intervals, coinciding with John Chambers' home leave.

When John Chambers was posted to the island town of Mombasa in 1925, he decided to send for his family. Arrangements were made and the family boarded a ship bound for Mombasa. But, while the ship was en route, John Chambers died. Dad, who by this time had been promoted to general manager of the Magadi Soda Company, had to go to Mombasa to meet John's family to break the news of his death, and thus met twenty year old Molly Chambers.

Grab a Spouse

In those days, Kenya was short of European women and, whenever a passenger ship arrived in Mombasa, there was a feverish haste by love-starved bachelors to meet the ship in hopes of capturing the choicest young ladies. Other bachelors hustled to the Nairobi railway station to meet the 'boat train' from Mombasa, hoping that there were still a few women, pretty or plain, that hadn't been swept away by those who had rushed down to Mombasa to meet the boat.

Although he certainly didn't have it in mind at the time, Dad's visit to Mombasa turned out to be a sort of grab-a-wife type expedition, as he was to marry Molly Chambers a couple of years later. They were married in Nairobi, and their 65 mile trip from Nairobi to Lake Naivasha for their honeymoon provided an insight into what Mum might expect in the future. But that is getting a bit ahead of the story.

Disciplinary action

During the time Dad served in the British Army, he had learned a great deal of pure Anglo-Saxon profanity. He claimed his fluency to have saved his life on one occasion, shortly after he became the General Manager of the Magadi Soda Company. As in many isolated communities, there was too much drinking at Magadi, and Dad had to make the rule that there was to be no drinking on duty. The man in charge of the boilers was an ex-British Army Royal Engineer who was generally bad tempered and a bully. He was strongly disliked by nearly everyone he met, and in his own paranoia, he carried a loaded British Army .303 rifle wherever he went.

One day, one of the African employees reported to Dad that the boiler man was drinking on duty, and Dad saw a good opportunity to dismiss the man, if the report proved true. So he hurried to the boiler room, and saw the man stoking the boiler with an open bottle of Haig & Haig Scotch whisky standing on the floor behind him. Dad picked up the bottle and tapped the man on the shoulder. He asked, "Is this yours?"

The old soldier spun round saying, "No, Sir. Nothing to do with me."

Dad threw the bottle at the wall, smashing it. "Well," he said "You won't mind if I do that with it."

The man grabbed his rifle, operated the bolt bringing a round up into the breach, and aimed the rifle at Dad, who let go a stream of British Army profanity, the likes of which the boiler man hadn't heard in years. And this from the lips of the General Manager, who was the last person the old veteran soldier expected to use such language. He dropped his rifle, and ran away, never to be seen again.

It is possible that he ran into the bush, and that a Masai tribesman bloodied his spear on the unfortunate drunk. It is also possible, but less probable, that he managed to walk for two or three days through the bush to get to Nairobi. The police were informed, but never turned up any evidence of a body or record of the man in Nairobi, or elsewhere.

Honeymoon

On their honeymoon trip to Naivasha, Dad drove his box-body car, the forerunner of the station wagon, up to the rim of the Great Rift Valley and down the escarpment to the Valley floor. The 1927 box-body cars were imported in basic form and then completed in Kenya by local auto body makers, using wood, angle iron and canvas. There were no doors for the driver and passenger, but the body was cut away to allow ease of access. Attached all round the roof were canvas curtains, normally kept rolled up, to provide protection against rain when unrolled, and fastened down onto turn-buckles fitted to the body. The curtains also reduced the number of locusts that could get into the car when passing through a swarm, which was a fairly common occurrence in those days. But the curtains didn't do much of a job against the ingress of rain when driving through tropical rainstorms.

These cars had to withstand the rough, dusty earth roads of the day. The roads were best described, in the dry seasons, as dry water courses consisting of washboard surfaces, joined together by pot holes, and ruts, covered in dust. During the wet season they turned into muddy tracks that demanded that the car be driven in the middle of the road on the top of the camber. Off the camber, the car would slide down into the ditch, there to remain until help arrived. Help came in the form of another motorist or a crowd of tribesmen who, for a few cents, would gladly push the car back onto the top of the camber. Payment before the push was required.

The road to the rim of the Great Rift Valley climbed up through ten or fifteen miles of red soil. This soil was renowned as a car stopper when wet. The surface became greasy on top of a hard surface, so it was like driving on buttered sheets of glass. So when Dad, with his new bride, drove up behind an elderly Kikuyu herdsman driving a dozen goats up the middle of the muddy road, he had to slow down to a walking pace, and gently ease the car through the slick mud, with rear wheels spinning. The gentleman herding his goats made no attempt to drive them to one side of the road. Nor was he able to go any faster than a slow walk, as he was clearly well past his athletic best.

Dad was not a patient man in such circumstances, and he finally blew up, loosing off a vitriolic stream of invective, which frightened Mum but had little effect on the old gentleman, or his goats. Eventually the procession reached a village, and the goats and their herder turned off to allow a fuming groom and startled bride to resume their travel at a more efficient speed.

The road down the escarpment into the Great Rift Valley was hazardous. It was narrow, rutted, stony and steep. On one side there was a 1,000 foot drop and, on the other, a near vertical bank. During wet weather it was nigh impossible to climb up the slippery road, and driving down was perilous. One drove as close to the bank as possible, and inched one's way down. Brakes were not what they are today, and driving in those days demanded intelligent anticipation at the best of times. The escarpment required negotiating gently as, in wet weather, it was possible to lock up all four wheels, but continue to slide on down the steep, muddy road.

As they progressed slowly down the track, a sleek bushbuck sprang from the bank on one side of the road onto the other side, and then disappeared down the cliff like a mountain goat. Dad drove slowly on, concentrating on the task of getting down the escarpment in one piece without any broken springs or burst tires. As they reached the spot from where the bushbuck had jumped, a leopard leapt through the car behind the astonished occupants. Dad was so startled, that he fired off another tirade, which only encouraged the leopard to chase faster after the bushbuck, and to scare Mum again. Mum always maintained that she learned a lot on their honeymoon - mainly the new-to-her Anglo Saxon swear words.

After their honeymoon, Mum and Dad went to Magadi to settle into married life. Mum was in her 23rd year and Dad was 38. His young bride was determined to make a success of her new position as the wife of the boss of one of Britain's largest operations in Kenya. A great opportunity to demonstrate her skills as a hostess presented itself all too soon.

3

The Prince of Wales

At that time, any VIP who visited the Colony was shown around some of the more important operations and facilities. So, when the Prince of Wales (PoW) visited Kenya in 1928, he was shown the Kenya and Uganda Railways and Harbors workshops in Nairobi, a large farm owned by Lord Delamere and the Magadi Soda company's operation at Lake Magadi.

His visit to Magadi came as a surprise and, on hearing of his sudden proposed visit with his cortege numbering in all 60 people, Mum went into a flat spin. She rushed towards the larder but changed direction and raced to find Dad.

"I can't manage sixty people," she spluttered.

"Don't worry," said Dad calmly. "We'll split 'em up into five groups. Each senior member of management will have to cope with twelve of 'em. So, you'll only have to deal with twelve - plus us, makes fourteen."

Mum rushed to the larder to discover she had nothing in sufficient quantity. She'd have to visit the one and only general store in Magadi. She, and the wives of the four other senior staff members, met at the store to find that the only things in sufficient quantity were sausages, potatoes and green peas.

The sausages were shared out. Fourteen per household. Mum's visions of a splendid formal dinner - to be served on her beautiful Spode chinaware illustrated with the 'Chelsea' pattern, her plated silverware and her crystal glasses - were jeopardized by the inadequacy of Magadi's Arab owned general store. She gave the servants a quick training course. The Prince of Wales was to be served first and Dad last - and various other important matters.

Who was this man, the Prince of Wales? Only the future King of England! Yes! It was he who was to become Edward VIII in 1936 for 326 days before his abdication in favor of Mrs. Wallis Simpson. He was a keen sportsman, and was to pay two visits to Kenya in order to shoot all the big game to which he could be put in close proximity. In order to justify his all-expenses-paid hunting trip, he was obliged to see those oft visited large operations of which the Colony's senior administrative staff (the Governor and his senior officers) were so proud. A successful visit might lead to a knighthood for the Governor, and other awards for his immediate subordinates.

And what are sausages? Well, there is nothing like a British sausage, familiarly known as a 'banger' and certainly not to be confused with an American sausage in flavor. It consists of ground, slightly spiced meat (pork or beef) encased in a tube of gut. It is eaten at breakfast with fried eggs and bacon, or at other meals with mashed potatoes, and usually, green peas. In England it is ubiquitous, but few Brits would expect bangers and mash (sausages and mashed potatoes) to be served at any of the Royal residences - or indeed at any smart English restaurant. But it is probably true to say that the common man in Britain would prefer to tuck into bangers, mash and green peas than any dish with a French name that is served at snooty, overpriced restaurants.

Bangers and mash, like fish and chips, which are best served as a take-away, wrapped in a sleazy tabloid newspaper, and soused with vinegar and salt to taste, are thought to be a staple diet amongst the less affluent classes in Britain. In fact, nearly all Brits at nearly all levels of society, gobble up bangers and mash or fish and chips with relish. Actually, many Brits refuse to travel abroad for fear of not being able to fill up, at regular intervals, with bangers and mash or fish and chips.

Mum was worried. How would the Prince of Wales suffer a meal of bangers and mash? But she had much to do. The house was cleaned throughout, a fresh roll of TP put in the loo, Dad's best monkey suit and shirt ironed, Mum's best evening dress pressed, and shoes cleaned and polished. Lamp shades and pictures on the walls were dusted, bath, sinks and faucets were cleaned and polished, the garden was watered, and Mum did her hair. No sooner had she done this, and straightened the cushions in the lounge, than the PoW and his cortege arrived, hot and dusty from his trip of sixty miles down the newly completed earth road from Nairobi to Magadi.

Dad and his assistants split up the party, and groups were led off to their allocated houses. Dad herded the PoW and his immediate attendants towards his house where Mum stood on the veranda waiting to put into effect the curtsey she had been practicing ever since she had learned of the PoW's imminent arrival.

After a couple of 'sundowners' on the veranda in the now cool evening zephyrs, Mum announced that dinner was about to be served, and the party trooped into the dining room. Dad showed the PoW to his place at the table, and then ensured that everyone else was seated in accordance with protocol. The PoW sat at one end of the table and Dad, as host, sat at the other. Mum's best crystal glassware, silver cutlery, white damask table linen, and ornate gravy boats presented a tasteful setting, lit by long red candles in elaborate candelabra.

Mum and Dad had received, as wedding gifts, sets of fairly respectable silver salvers and the servants now filed in with the bangers in one salver, the mash in another and the peas in a third. The servants were dressed in their livery of white *kanzus* (long cotton robes) with red cummerbunds embroidered with intricate designs in gold thread, and red fezes with black tassels. They went round the table from person to person in the sequence in which Mum had instructed them. On seeing the bangers, mash and green peas, the PoW exclaimed with much enthusiasm, "By Jove! Bangers and mash! One of my favorites!"

Was he trying to put Mum at her ease? Or did he really have a 'common' taste? Perhaps his obsession for Mrs Simpson a few years later confirmed that he had only a 'common' taste, but I like to think that he was really a gentleman, who had enjoyed simple fare at al fresco meals in palace gardens, and had acquired a taste for the dishes so popular with his future subjects.

Anyway, to show his enthusiasm, the PoW took two bangers. The servants were doing their job admirably and, as good servants should, kept their eyes averted. So, the man serving the bangers was unaware of the fact that when he thrust the salver over Dad's shoulder, there was no lone banger left. Dad half turned and looked up at the servant, who must have seen Dad's upturned face out of the corner of his eye. The servant looked down and saw the empty salver. He took a pace to the rear, and surveyed the table, immediately spotting two bangers on the future King of England's plate.

He moved swiftly round to the other end of the table, reached over the PoW's shoulder, deftly grasped a banger between thumb and forefinger, and put it neatly in the salver. He moved back down the table and, with panache, presented the banger to Dad. It is quite probable that Mum nearly had a heart attack, but Dad could only roar with laughter - as did everyone else.

The stiff formality was dissipated and the party went with a swing. Naturally, the silver plated salver was for-evermore treated with special regard. I now have the salver, which has been in regular use but now has large patches from where the silver has been polished away.

PoW visits the Delamere farm

When the PoW visited Lord Delamere's farm, afternoon tea was served on a well tended green lawn surrounded by neatly clipped hedges. Everybody who was anybody was there. Aristocratic looking ladies moved graciously about the lawn in floral frocks and big hats. The men looked a little uncomfortable in unsuitable suits with stiff collars and ties, trying not to break wind - loudly.

Everyone had tea in a cup and saucer in one hand and a small plate of little triangular white cucumber sandwiches in the other. This is an odd English upper-class tradition. It is not actually possible to either drink one's tea or eat the sandwiches while both hands are so engaged and, by the time a place has been found to put things down, the tea is cold and the sandwiches have begun to curl at the edges.

Suddenly one of Lord Delamere's Masai herdsmen ran onto the lawn. He was dressed in traditional Masai garb. A blanket thrown casually over one shoulder, a spear in one hand and a shield in the other. Nothing else. There were a few little ladylike screams, whether of appreciation or embarrassment, we are not told. A gentleman was heard to declare, "I say!" which is a typically English gentleman's remark on such occasions. After a few words with Lord Delamere, the Masai herdsman turned and ran off, his family jewels dangling in the bright afternoon sun for all to see.

Lord Delamere turned to the PoW. "Terribly sorry about that," he said, "a steer has been found dead. Probably killed by a lion. My herdsman was just reporting to me."

"Don't apologize, my dear Delamere. Please don't apologize. Think nothing of it. Life has to go on and I'm certainly not here to stop it." The PoW was effusive. "I say,

Delamere," he continued, "I must say, I do admire your servants' livery!"

To hunt or to ....

Two years later, in 1930, the PoW returned to kill a few more wild animals. This time he came with a younger brother, Henry, Duke of Gloucester. The PoW hadn't, as yet, fallen for Wallis, but his reputation for being sportive, as well as being a sportsman, was well known. As a result, willing ladies of the 'White Mischief' clique abounded. It's possible that the PoW wanted Henry to enjoy both the hunt after game as well as the joy of being the prey of a delectable, delinquent dazzler. Debauchery was on the horizon.

An outcome was that a singularly able young lady, Beryl, found herself to be in the family way. This matter was kept secret. Those in the know, alleged the father was Henry, but it might be supposed that this allegation was to curb the parental liability of the future monarch. The PoW, having no wife or children - as far as was known - might have had to accept the bastard as his first born, and the effect of this on the succession to the throne would have caused chaos. Suffice it to say that Henry, Duke of Gloucester, was designated liable. An annuity of 2,000 pounds was settled on the lady. Being a person of her word, she never mentioned the matter. The bastard son was raised in Britain where he lived until, at the age of fifty-two, he was killed in a car crash. His mother, the famous Beryl Markham, after renouncing her misconception in Britain, returned to Kenya to become an ace light aircraft pilot, initially under the tutelage of Denys Finch Hatton. In 1936 she was the first person to fly non-stop across the Atlantic, east to west, from London to Nova Scotia. In 1939 she settled in California, and wrote a book - 'West with the Night'. On her return to Kenya in 1952, she resumed an earlier occupation, and became a renowned and successful horse breeder and trainer, a business in which she had excelled as a young woman in her early 20's. She was a lady of great talent, spirit and character.

Beryl and the Coupe d'etat

In her later years, Beryl became just a little imperious and irascible. In 1980, a farcical attempt at a coupe d'etat was staged in Kenya. Road blocks were set up by the police and army all over Nairobi. Those manning the road blocks were not exactly sure of what they were supposed to be doing.

Beryl was to luncheon with a friend at the Muthaiga Country Club on the other side of Nairobi. She set off in her little car, but was stopped at a road block. Being in a bit of a hurry, she became testy when, in her opinion, she was held up unnecessarily by a bunch weapon waving idiots in uniform, who didn't seem to understand that she wasn't the least bit interested in their coupe d'etat.

Patience lost, she sped off followed by a fusillade of shots. A bullet grazed her chin and this only served to raise the ire of this 78 year old lady. What the rather poorly trained and overly excited men thought they were doing, will never be known. They quite likely only wanted an excuse to shoot somebody, and an elderly lady would serve well enough as a trophy.

As Beryl drove on, she decided to report the matter. This she did at a police station five miles from where the incident took place. She was furious and bleeding from her gunshot wound. Her angry tirade at the police station confused the officers in that establishment, and they became as dopey as those who had shot her. So Beryl stormed out, and went to have lunch with her friend, dabbing the blood from her chin, still enraged by the absolute imbecility of the police.

4

A Right Charlie , or The Great White Hunter

Another keen sportsman who came to Kenya was a noted American. His arrival was heralded by much publicity, for this man had shot almost every sort of animal in the United States and Canada with either a rifle or with bow and arrow. Coinciding with his arrival, some of his exploits were reported in the local press. Back in the U.S. he had a house full of animal head trophies, and claimed many records. He was to visit Magadi. At that time the area abounded with all sorts of game. Rhinos were particularly common, and so were various types of gazelle and antelopes. And, where there were such animals, there were also lions and leopards.

After several years in Africa, hunting was no longer an attractive sport for Dad. He now shot only when necessary. A marauding rhino or buffalo. A cattle killing lion or leopard. An animal wounded by a Masai spear. Sick and old animals no longer able to feed. These had to be dealt with. Now the American hunter demanded that he be escorted around the area and the job fell to a disgruntled Dad. I can only suppose that the man was well connected and that Dad had been given orders that he personally should escort the American, Charlie.

The term 'white hunter' refers to any professional hunter, regardless of color, recognized by the Professional Hunters' Association and licensed by the Game Department to take clients on hunting safaris. He takes his paying clients into designated hunting areas to shoot for sport, and has to ensure that the client has bought hunting licenses from the Game Department for every type of animal he wishes to kill.

Charlie must have thought that a white hunter referred to a white man properly kitted out and suitably armed. Charlie wore snow white drill safari suits, a snow white solar topi, snow white kid-skin leather boots and had enough firearms to equip an army. Of course, the firearms were all of the finest quality. He arrived wearing his whites - what else? Charlie was a white 'white hunter'. He was slightly dusty after his road trip from Nairobi and was eager to slake his thirst with a few Scotches on the rocks while he related some of his hunting stories to anyone who cared to listen.

Early the following morning Charlie was keen to be off and so was Dad. Magadi gets very hot in the mid-day sun. They set off in Dad's box-body car which Charlie referred to as a 'hunting car'. Dad soon determined that Charlie's eyesight was not perfect, and that he was too vain to wear spectacles. Dad drove down a rocky track away from the lake. The country was dry. The sun was bright. The track was dusty and rough. On the side of a rocky ridge, at a distance of 500 paces, Dad spotted three animals. He stopped the car and trained his field glasses on the possible trophies.

"What is it? What is it?" asked the excited Charlie.

"Well I'll be darned," said Dad in utter astonishment. "Blue Eland."

"Blue Eland?" queried Charlie.

"Yes," whispered Dad. "Very, very rare and very, very timid. Can you see them?"

"No," whispered Charlie excitedly. "No. I can't see them. Where are they? Blue Eland, did you say? I'd like to get one of those. Very rare did you say? Any of them with good horns?"

"Yeah! The one highest on the ridge looks like a record. Never seen such a monster."

"Where? Where?" Charlie's, excitement was now at fever pitch.

Dad directed Charlie's myopic eyes to the animal highest on the ridge. Charlie finally saw the Blue Eland amongst the shimmering rocks.

"You'll have to stalk in from here. Hands and knees stuff, I'm afraid. You'll have to make for that rocky mound and shoot from there. Be very careful. Blue Eland are really timid and have tremendous eyesight."

"Don't tell me how to approach a timid animal," snapped Charlie in a hoarse whisper. "I know what I'm doing!"

Charlie climbed out of the 'hunting car', lay down in the dust and began to wriggle towards the mound of rocks a few hundred paces away. When he reached the rocks, he lay panting for several minutes and then took aim with a .470 double barreled elephant rifle, and shot the animal dead. A previously unseen Masai herdsman sprang up from among the rocks and ran over to the dead animal. Charlie raced up the ridge to make sure the savage didn't mess with his trophy. Dad, who had quietly walked along behind Charlie as he wriggled through the dust, arrived a moment after Charlie.

There lay a very dead, miserable little Masai donkey. And there stood a very irate Masai tribesman. The Masai had just lost the very best donkey he'd ever had. In fact it was the very best donkey in Masailand. In fact it was the very best donkey in the whole damned world!

"Why did you kill my donkey?" shouted the angry Masai in Swahili. "Who would want to kill a donkey? What sort of a man are you?"

Charlie couldn't understand the questions, but it was obvious that the Masai was infuriated.

"I thought it was a Blue Eland explained Charlie. "You see I'm a white hunter."

Charlie gestured to his now not-so-white safari suit. The Masai thought he was being offered the clothing and became angrier. Dad intervened.

"You'd better give him some money. He wants compensation."

Charlie dived into his pocket and pulled out a wad of bills. He peeled off a good number and proffered them to the Masai. The Masai snatched them, and the rest of the wad. He seemed to mellow slightly. Gratified, he spat on the ground. The wad disappeared into the blanket he wore over one shoulder, and he sauntered off apparently mollified. He whistled to his other donkeys, and led them away down the rocky slope.

Charlie heaved a sigh of relief and stared at the carcass of the most expensive dead donkey in the world. He tried to brush the dirt off his safari suit but it seemed particularly well ingrained. And the suit was ripped in a few places by the thorns and rocks through which he had crawled.

"Do you want the head for a trophy?" asked Dad innocently.

Charlie gave Dad a look that would have curdled milk. "No!" he snapped, "and I don't want to hear the word donkey ever again!"

"OK. OK," said Dad, "I just thought that you might want to hang his head on a wall."

"Well, I don't!" snarled Charlie. "I had to give that bastard a thousand shillings. What's a donkey worth in these parts?"

"Well," said Dad, "a live one would cost you about 4 shillings. But if you shoot one, it'll cost you a bit more."

Not having seen the Masai until he leapt up from the rocks, Dad had thought the donkey to be a feral animal of

31

which there were far too many in the area at the time. He would never intentionally have allowed Charlie to shoot an animal that was a man's possession. But his mistake was mitigated by the over-generous compensation that the Masai had appropriated from Charlie.

Much to Dad's exasperation, Charlie was keen to do some more shooting - but no more donkeys, and to hell with the mythical blue eland. So, the next morning saw Dad and Charlie setting off again in the 'hunting car'. Charlie was wearing a fresh white hunter's suit. The one he'd worn yesterday was dirty and torn but would fit in very well with some of his stories about white hunting in Africa. Today Charlie was cradling a beautifully engraved double .500 Express rifle made by Rigby, a top English gun maker. His safari suit had loops on the left breast and these were filled with .500 rounds. Charlie was ready for anything.

Dad drove slowly along rutted, rocky tracks. The sun blazed down and already there was a heat haze. The rocks shimmered, and the only sign of life was the occasional little bird flitting from one thorn bush to another, or a vulture circling lazily in the deep blue sky. Suddenly Dad brought the hunting car to a stop and pointed.

"Lion," he breathed.

"Where? Where?" whispered the excited Charlie with bated breath.

"There," said Dad pointing. "Behind that small bush. You can just see the top of his head and ears sticking above the bush."

"Oh yes. I've got him spotted." Charlie began to take aim. Dad knocked the rifle up.

"You can't shoot from the car," he told the bewildered Charlie. "Not sporting. Not allowed. You'll have to get out and stalk up a bit closer. This heat haze makes accurate shooting difficult. You'll have to get up really close. Think you can do it?"

"Yeah! I'm not scared." whispered Charlie.

"OK," said Dad, "So long as you keep low. Don't let him see you or he might charge."

"Really?" Charlie was somewhat apprehensive.

"If he charges, for goodness sake shoot straight." advised Dad.

Charlie sat in the car for a few seconds wondering if he really did want to shoot a lion. Eventually he slid from the car to the ground, and started his wriggle across the dirt, through the thorn scrub and over the rocks to a convenient earth bank some 40 yards from his prey. As he neared the bush behind which his target lay, he could see less of the animal. Any closer and he'd have no target.

He aimed his Rigby double barreled .500 Express rifle at the crown of the animal's head, dropped his aim a couple of inches knowing that the heavy slug would not be diverted by a few twigs and leaves. He squeezed the trigger. There was a roar from the heavy rifle, and Charlie leapt to his feet. He raced towards where his trophy lay dead.

Now this was a silly thing to do. A lion has a very low, sloping brow, and many a bullet has ricocheted off the skull of a lion, merely stunning it. Dad leapt forward after Charlie. He had again been walking quietly behind the wriggling Charlie as he stalked up to the mound.

Dad's Mauser 10.75 mm bolt action rifle had a hair trigger which must have caught on a twig. There was an explosion and the rifle was nearly torn from Dad's grasp. Charlie stopped in his tracks. Dad circled slowly until he could see the dead animal.

Charlie had blown away a hyena. Mistaking a hyena for a lion has been a common error, and this hyena was an exceptionally large one. Charlie's .500 bullet had removed the crown of the animal's head. Dad, too shaken by his rifle having fired accidentally, had little to say. He back-tracked and found the spot where the bullet had hit the ground - within an inch of a heel mark made by Charlie's boot. Whether Charlie's boot had been there when the bullet hit the ground is unknown, but Dad was more than a little shaken. He went back to where Charlie was standing over his trophy.

"Never run up to a dangerous animal. No matter how sure you are that it is dead. You must always re-load and then circle round until you can see the carcass. Approach slowly, and watch to see if the animal is still breathing. If it is, give it another shot."

Charlie was contrite and seemed to think that Dad had fired his rifle to attract his attention in order to stop his rush at the carcass.

"Sorry." said Charlie. "Got a bit over excited."

"Yes, well I suppose we all do when we are beginners." Dad was talking to one of the greatest of all white hunters.

"Do you want the head as a trophy ?" Dad inquired innocently.

"No! I do not!" snapped the Great White Hunter testily. "And I never want to hear the word hyena again!"

Charlie wasn't getting any trophies, but he now had two dirty, torn white safari suits and these were almost as good as trophies.

Charlie was content, but became excited again, a few days later, when a Masai tribesman came to tell Dad that a lion was killing cattle. A goat had been killed that very night. The lion had leapt over the thorn fence of the *manyatta*. This is a temporary Masai village, enclosed in a thick, high thorn fence. It includes a corral for livestock. The lion had taken a goat and leapt back over the fence.

Dad would have to try to kill the lion for, if they become livestock killers, it indicates that the lion has been disabled or is too ill or old to hunt with the pride. And once a livestock killer, always a livestock killer - unless it takes to man-eating.

Dad loaded up the 'hunting car', and prepared to drive off with the Masai tribesman as guide. Charlie insisted that he come along too. He was armed with a bolt action magazine rifle, a .404 caliber by Jeffreys of England, and a bottle of Haig and Haig whisky by Haig and Haig of Scotland.

When they reached the *manyatta*, it was clear what had happened. After the lion had jumped back over the fence with the goat in his jaws, the Masai warriors in the *manyatta*, having been awakened by the terrified livestock, had rushed out into the darkness, and had driven the lion away with shouts. The lion hadn't even started to eat the goat.

Dad had a steel gin trap. This device consists of spring loaded jaws which are forced open against the strong spring. Between the open jaws is a plate which, when depressed, allows the jaws to snap together with great force trapping the paw of the animal. This type of trap is cruel but effective. Fastened to the trap was a strong chain which was attached to a tree, and the carcass of the goat was placed by the trap.

A wooden *machan* (platform from which to shoot) was built in the tree. The idea was to sit up on the *machan* to await the return of the lion, and dispatch it with a well placed shot. The trap was set so that, if the animal was caught in it, there was no possibility of it dashing off if the bullet was not well placed. Finally, Dad set up a tent 150 yards way from the carcass.

"With all the activity today, its very unlikely that the lion will return tonight," he explained to Charlie. "So, we may as well get some sleep, and sit up over the carcass tomorrow night."

"Well," said Charlie, "if you don't mind, I'll sit up tonight." Taking his .404 Jeffreys in one hand and his bottle of Haig and Haig in the other, he disappeared towards the tree in the twilight. Dad turned in, kept his loaded 10.75 rifle beside him, and left the oil lamp alight with the wick turned down.

At 4.00 in the morning all hell, as they say, broke loose. Snarls were interrupted by shot after shot. Dad, who had remained fully clothed and booted, grabbed his rifle, and ran through the moonlight toward the tree. As he rounded a bush, all was revealed.

Dancing drunkenly on the *machan*, Charlie was firing shot after shot at the stars. A leopard, caught in the trap, was trying to leap onto the platform but the chain was too short. The poor animal was snarling with pain and rage. The only time the shots stopped was when Charlie's magazine needed reloading. Despite his condition, Charlie seemed to be able to reload with considerable alacrity.

In the moonlight, Dad snapped off a shot, and managed only to shoot off the tail of the leaping leopard. A second shot killed the poor animal. After two more shots at the stars, Charlie's rifle was again empty. Silence. Charlie realised that something had happened. He peered down at the tailless leopard. Then he saw Dad.

"Hic. Gorrim, hic," slurred Charlie with satisfaction. He had another look at the leopard, decided it was really dead, handed his rifle down to Dad, took a last swig of Haig and Haig, passed Dad the nearly empty bottle, and climbed down from the tree. He looked down at the leopard, and hitched up his pants. "Hic. Gorrim, hic," he mumbled with satisfaction.

"Bed," blurted Charlie and staggered towards the tent, collapsing into bed with a final, "Hic. Gorrim, hic," before passing out.

Charlie slept until 11.30 am and came out of the tent red eyed. Dad was sitting quietly outside.

"What happened?" asked Charlie.

Without replying, Dad got up and led the way to the tree. Charlie stared at the dead, tailless leopard.

"Got him," said a satisfied Charlie. Then he saw that the leopard had lost its tail. He sighed.

"Do you want the skin for a trophy?" asked Dad innocently.

"Useless. No tail." muttered Charlie and stalked off despondently.

The Masai had been mistaken. It was not a lion that had started raiding cattle corrals. The dead leopard was aged and, being no longer capable of hunting wild game, had taken to domestic stock killing.

The platform was taken down and the boards, trap, tent and rest of the kit were reloaded into the 'hunting car'. Charlie wasn't able to help much as he was nursing a hangover. On the way back he asked "What happened?" Dad started to tell him but realised that Charlie wasn't listening. When they got back to our home, Mum asked Charlie how things had gone

"Got him," declared Charlie and went to his room to sleep off his hangover.

The following morning Charlie appeared for the first time dressed in an ordinary cotton shirt and pants. All three of his white hunter's safari suits were torn and dirty. He had torn the third suit clambering up and down the tree. They were to be his trophies. "If you don't mind, I'll push on back to Nairobi," Charlie announced. Nobody objected to his plan.

Months later, someone showed Dad a hunting journal. Charlie had sold the story of his exploits in Africa. 'Unfortunately,' the exaggerated article read, 'all the trophies were lost when they were being loaded onto the ship at Mombasa. The case in which they were packed fell from the crane down between the ship and the wharf, and could not be recovered.' There was a picture of Charlie, double .500 Express rifle in hand, wearing one of his torn and grubby white Hunter's safari suits.

5

A Quiet American

Not all American hunters that visited Kenya were Charlies. Years later I met one who taught me a thing or two. This was at a time when I was confident that I knew as much bushcraft as many an expert. It was in 1955 when I was officer-in-charge of the Tracker Wing of The East Africa Battle School. I was asked to escort Roy, a keen American hunter, into the forest of Mount Kenya. Roy wanted to bag a good sized buffalo. It was well known to many hunters that the Mount Kenya forest was the best place to find buffalo with above average horns. But the forest was the haunt of Mau-Mau terrorists and was out of bounds to all except the Security Forces. Roy must have had considerable influence with the Kenya Game Department.

I met Roy the evening he arrived at a Nanyuki hotel where he had booked in. He was a slim, wiry man of small stature. His face was craggy, which failed to conceal laugh lines. And there was a clear indication of a determination in those steel blue eyes. His greeting was friendly, and we made arrangements to meet early the following morning. I asked what rifle he intended to use, and was happy when he showed me a .425 double barreled rifle manufactured by Cogswell Harrison. He handled it confidently and safely.

He was waiting when I arrived to collect him the following morning a little before 5.30 am. I had borrowed a Landrover, and we set off for a friend's farm some ten miles away. There we left the vehicle, and walked into the forest a couple of miles to the east. Gray dawn was breaking as we entered the forest, and we sat and waited for the light to improve.

"Hey! Have a look at this," said Roy pointing to what appeared to be a scuff mark amongst the rotting leaves. "I reckon a hare heard us coming and scampered away."

I was impressed that Roy had spotted the sign, which was by no means easily seen. I inspected the marks. There was no doubt that he was correct. I hadn't even seen the marks, and began to realise that this fellow, had a good pair of eyes and used them. I had never taken much notice of small animal tracks. I thought about this for some time, and realised that I didn't know as much as I thought I did. If the hare had been startled, what about other animals? What about buffalo? It was as though a missed chapter of a book had been opened, and the more I thought about it, the more I realised that there is a lot to learn about small creatures.

I found a lone buffalo hoof-print. This was lucky as the chances were that he was an old animal, cast out by a younger bull from his herd, and this could also mean that he was a big animal. I cast around for tracks. Yes, there they were. Fresh spoor of a big bull. His hoof-prints were big, but it didn't necessarily follow that his horns were large. I showed Roy the tracks and asked him to follow them. After studying them for a few moments he began to track slowly.

"You can follow faster if you like." I said. "He'll go for a while and then begin to eat. You'll see where he's nipped the grass. That's when you have to be more careful."

Roy tracked more quickly. After a mile or two, he saw the first sign that the buffalo was thinking about breakfast. He attracted my attention to a difference in the length of the stride of the left and right forelegs. The buffalo was lame. Roy spotted nibbled grass.

"He will probably settle down to graze almost immediately," I whispered and Roy nodded his understanding. We proceeded at a slower pace. He spotted the light gray shape of the buffalo through the undergrowth and signaled to me by hand, not wishing to alert the animal. I moved up beside Roy.

"I'll leave this to you," I whispered and slowly crouched down in the long grass.

Roy turned to study the situation. With the utmost caution he began to circle to his right, opening up the target. After fifty paces, he stopped and stood stock still. He was now within twenty yards of the buffalo. Finally, as though reluctant, he slowly raised his rifle, took careful aim, and squeezed the trigger. There was a roar, and the buffalo dropped dead. Cautiously, Roy approached the big bull, and then relaxed. I stood up, brushed the twigs from my pants, and walked over to Roy.

"Classic," I said referring to the way in which Roy had tackled the hunt. He was happy.

"Thanks," he said quietly, gazing at the buffalo which had bigger horns than I had first thought. Then we saw a dreadful suppurating wound low on the buffalo's right foreleg. This was the cause of the animal's lameness and was almost certainly the result of the fight that had ended with the buffalo being ousted from his herd.

I thought it prudent to see if we had attracted the attention of any Mau Mau. I told Roy to stay where he was while I circled the area, but found no evidence of any terrorists. We covered the carcass with brushwood, and hurried back to the farm to collect an expert skinner. We were able to drive the Landrover well up into the forest and, leaving it with a guard, we hurried to skin the carcass and cut up the meat. We loaded the vehicle and went back to the farm where the skinner completed his job. The hide was carefully rolled up and we headed back to Nanyuki. Roy was withdrawn and seemed overcome by a heavy sadness.

He offered to pay me for my services. I refused, so Roy bought us a beer and then decided to return to Nairobi immediately. He must have arrived there late at night. I knew that he was keen to have the buffalo hide taken care of, but there was something else that was absorbing his thoughts. Some weeks later I received a photo of the mounted buffalo head with a letter from Roy saying thanks for escorting him on his last hunt with a rifle. He had been able to complete his trophy collection with a fine specimen, but from now on, he would shoot only with a camera.

Misidentification

It is easy to make mistakes in the identification of animals out on the hot dry plains when the shimmering heat haze blurs things as close as fifty paces or even less. I had a narrow escape which will be with me all my life. When I was about thirteen, my school friend Billy asked me to go hunting with him. He had a .22 caliber rifle, and we had found that, if shot from close range, say twenty-five yards, it was possible to bag a Thomson's gazelle (Tommy), which are good eating. We set off on our bicycles to what is now the Nairobi National Park, which was a mere five miles from Billy's home. Apart from Billy's .22, we were armed with heavy hunting knives, and plenty of enthusiasm.

We rode slowly along a smooth earth track, and I spotted, through the shimmering heat haze, a lone Tommy just as he disappeared behind a clump of bushes. We quickly dismounted and, crouching low, we moved quietly to a waist-high whistling thorn tree about 20 yards from the bush that was now hiding the Tommy. Slowly we stood up, and peered over the tree just in time to see the Tommy through the bush about to come out into the open. I raised the rifle,

41

closed my left eye and took aim at where I thought his shoulder would clear the bush. Billy slid up beside me and gently pushed the rifle up.

"It's a lioness," he breathed. I opened my eye and took a good look to see a lioness move slowly from behind the bush. She looked enormous from such a short distance, and the .22 rifle in my hands seemed little more than a toy.

Had I squeezed off a shot from the .22, it would have only enraged the lioness, and we would have been done for. I was sure that I hadn't mistaken a lioness for a Tommy in the heat haze. I expect that the Tommy was some distance further away, and that the Tommy knew he was safe, as the lioness wasn't hunting. Animals can sense whether a predator is hunting, I presume by body language.

Billy and I stood stock still, hoping that the lioness wouldn't see us. The little whistling thorn tree seemed suddenly very insubstantial, and I felt that we were virtually out in the open. Slowly the lioness strolled on and, as she drew away from us, we made 'a tactical withdrawal', which is what the British army calls a panic stricken retreat. We got on our bicycles and pedaled for all we were worth. We still had the .22 rifle and our heavy hunting knives, but the enthusiasm had waned, and had been replaced by prudence. We rode back to Billy's home to play an exciting game of chess.

Myrtle and the big gray thing

It was an American lady who was the least interested in the wonderful wildlife that inhabits Kenya. There are some folk for whom wildlife is only of passing interest. They are more interested in the natives and their culture, but nearly everyone has at least a flicker of interest in the animals and birds.

Not Myrtle. She was one of those new-comers who display presumptive airs that they are the heirs presumptive to white leadership in ex-colonies. Not for them the supposed proud arrogance of the idle, raunchy, dissolute settlers of old that was the perception of many throughout the world of Hollywood and its idolizers. Myrtle would show the poor down-trodden natives of Kenya that she was respectful of and deeply interested in their supposedly unsophisticated ways. She oozed the virtue of humility toward their arts. She was totally absorbed in studying the natives, and identified with them by learning their dances, and trying to copy their wood carvings. She actually disliked wild animals, and those who sought to conserve wildlife and the habitat. In particular, she disliked the local Game Warden, Rodney, who epitomized the most passionate of wild animal lovers, and was fervent in the protection of the animals and their environment.

Myrtle had rented a house bordering a game park, and was pestered by lions roaring at night, gazelles eating her flowers, and all sorts of other animals that used her yard as a restroom. She complained incessantly to Rodney who, though polite, made it obvious that, in his view, animals come before humans, and she would have to put up with a few inconveniences if she wanted to enjoy the wildlife. Which she Didn't.

One morning Myrtle was painting with watercolors at her dining table. The picture was of an African village with grass thatched mud and wattle huts and women and children in colorful clothes working in the fields - no animals. She looked up, and to her horror saw a wild animal in her back garden. She immediately grabbed the phone, and dialed the Game Warden's number .

"I've got one of your animals in my back garden," she exploded when Rodney answered.

"Well, what do you expect me to do with it?" he asked querulously.

"Get rid of it," she snapped.

"What sort of an animal is it?"

"How should I know? But it's one of yours."

"Can you see it?"

"Yes. Come and chase it away." Myrtle's impatience was growing rapidly.

"What color is it?"

"Sort of gray."

"How big is it?"

"I don't know. It's huge. I can't see the whole damned thing. I'm looking through my dining room window and its too big to see the whole of it."

"What's it doing?" asked Rodney.

"It's pulling up my prize cauliflowers with its tail and, if I told you where its stuffing them, you wouldn't believe me!"

6

Doc Forbes's Bedside Manner

Because Magadi was so isolated, the Magadi Soda Company employed a full time general medical practitioner. Doc Forbes was one of those sons of Scotland who, though born of humble circumstances, was recognized to be a clever boy, and was sent to university to study medicine. After qualifying in 1885, Doc went out to South Africa. His first practice was the Transvaal Province, which has an area of approximately 100,500 sq. miles. It was the perimeter of the Transvaal Province that was his practice. He lived in an ox-drawn covered wagon similar to those used by the early settlers in America to take themselves and their families West. It took Doc a year to complete one circuit of his practice. Ladies timed the birth of their children for the time that Doc would be in their neighborhood.

Later, as more doctors went out to South Africa, the ladies no longer had to plan their families with such care. They could be careless, and let passion rear its ugly head.

So later, when constant traveling round the Transvaal became tedious, Doc took the job of Company Doctor at Magadi, but found there was too little to do. Most of his attention was given to Masai tribesmen who had had fights with friends, or had battled with a wild animal. Such incidents produced wounds from torn ear lobes to far more serious injuries from being mauled by a lion or gored by a buffalo or rhino. When the road to Magadi from Nairobi was completed, the company's employees were able to get full medical attention and proper hospitalization. So, Doc went to Nairobi to start a practice there.

As the son of a crofter, and having practiced it the Transvaal where his patients were the wives of Boer farmers, Doc had never found it necessary to develop a bed-side-manner. Nor did his practice at Magadi demand this skill, and in Nairobi, his patients were at the rough end of the social scale, so he got by with his exceptional medical know-how rather than through tact. But, in time, Doc found his practice waning. He thought about this over several months, and came to the conclusion that younger doctors were arriving in the Colony, and they had that extra polish.

Doc bought a book on how to develop a bed-side-manner, and practiced in private. On the day he decided to bring his newly developed skill out of the closet, he was to pay a weekly visit to the bed-ridden wife of a railway fireman. Like most of his patients, Mrs Green had no social graces. She called a spade a bloody shovel.

Doc walked in wearing a new business suit, white shirt and tie. He had forsaken his comfortable old boots for polished shoes. He had a new doctor's bag, and his hair was neatly brushed and slicked down with a scented pomade.

Unctuously wringing his hands he asked, "My dear Mrs Green, how are you today? Very well, I hope. You are looking wonderful, as usual."

Mrs Green's eyes opened wide in amazement.

"Now. Let's have a look at you, my dear," Doc continued. "Ah yes. You have been looking after yourself properly and taking your pills. Yes, you are one of my best patients, dear Mrs Green." Her eyes opened wider.

"I do so enjoy my little visits to you, Mrs Green," Doc continued to gush.

"Doc. You're drunk!" exploded Mrs Green. So ended Doc's attempt at a bed-side-manner.

Just too isolated

After a road had been built from Nairobi to Magadi, the only general store was able to offer a greater range of foodstuffs. A new water pipe supplied good, potable water from a source fifty miles away, and the company had engaged Doc Forbes to provide medical attention for the Company's employees. Mum thought Magadi had become sufficiently civilized for family life and my sister, Elizabeth, was born in February 1928 and I arrived on the scene in December 1930.

But Magadi was not the best spot to raise a family. It was too hot for the refrigerators of those days to keep food fresh. A full range of family needs was still not available. The drive to Nairobi was a car breaker, and a family could be stranded. In addition, there had been a tragic death, and a few foolish accidents with rifles that had not had serious consequences, but were enough to challenge Mum's views on Magadi as a place to raise a young family.

Sudden Death in a Whirlwind

My Dad was walking down to the mill one day when a whirlwind suddenly erupted, tearing at branches and swirling dust into the air. An African worker was walking toward Dad when the whirlwind tore the corrugated iron roof from a shed, and whipped it round in an arc that severed the man's leg. Even before he fell to the ground, the iron sheeting whirled around a second time, and severed the other leg. By the time Dad could summon help, the poor man was dead.

Near Misses

There was a lot of game in the Magadi area in those days, and even walking around the small residential area had its dangers. All the men constantly carried rifles, and most of them were experienced in shooting dangerous wildlife when necessary.

One day Dad had been out and, as was his habit, he carried his 10.75 mm sporting rifle. My parents were to have guests for drinks - sundowners - that evening and the padre had already arrived, and was sitting on the verandah enjoying a cold beer. Mum was doing her hair at her dressing table when Dad came in. He sat on the end of the bed and operated the bolt of his rifle half a dozen times to eject the round in the breech and clear the magazine. He snapped the bolt shut and squeezed the trigger. The last round had not ejected and the rifle went off, sending the bullet through the comb in my mother's hair, and knocking out three large bricks from the wall. The alarmed padre rushed in to see a cloud of dust and smoke. He smiled at Mum's reaction.

"Tsk, tsk," said Mum. "Now you've wakened the babies!"

On another occasion there was a Sunday cocktail party and people were sitting around in folding chairs enjoying a cool drink in the sun. One man had brought his rifle with him. He raised his foot, took careful aim at it and squeezed the trigger. The 'empty' gun went off, the hollow point bullet passed between the bones of his foot and went off into space. That hollow point bullet should have broken up and torn his foot to shreds, but for some unknown reason it only made a neat hole through his foot between the many bones. He was walking again in a few days.

Nairobi via Carshalton Beeches

Mum came to the conclusion that Magadi, for many reasons, was not the place to raise infants. Dad resigned, and took the family to England. He bought a house in Carshalton Beeches, south of London, and started to look for a job. But 1931 was not a good time to look for employment as the Great Depression was well under way. Nine months later, in 1932, we were all back in Kenya.

Dad was fortunate to find employment of any kind. The world's economies were in chaos, and jobs were extremely difficult to find. There was a gold rush in the Kakamega area of western Kenya. Dad's employer, Mitchell Cotts, sent him up to Kakamega to determine whether it was worthwhile importing heavy mining machinery. The job necessitated Dad having to be away from his family for extended periods. He therefore determined to find other employment more appropriate to his experience and training, nearer home as soon as possible.

Being a little over eighteen months old and being unqualified to take any responsibilities, I was unaware of all this. So my opinion was not asked in any of these important matters. Dad took a house a mile or so from the center of Nairobi on Girouard Road (now Ralph Bunche Road). The house was of stone with a corrugated iron roof. Nairobi, being at an altitude of nearly 6,000 feet above sea level, can become quite cold and most houses have fireplaces. Our house had one in the lounge. I mention this as it was to play an important part in my becoming aware of the world.

Up to the age of about twenty months, I was not really mentally switched on. I remember nothing of our short sojourn in England nor of the return sea voyage. But my memories do go back to when I was very young, and I clearly remember some events that took place at the Girouard Road house when I was between two and three years of age.

A bit too much warmth

Which event it was that triggered my mental processes, I don't know. But it is quite likely the occasion when my Aunt Ada came to our house, dressed to go to the theater with my parents. My maternal grandmother, Mary Chambers, also came with Aunt Ada to look after Elizabeth, my sister, and me. Grandma, Aunt Ada and we children were in the lounge while my parents finished getting ready for their night out. Ada looked wonderful in a long cream colored taffeta gown with a fine net over-skirt.

The evening was cold, the fire was roaring, and we gathered around its warmth. Suddenly Ada burst into flames. In an instant the net skirt was ablaze. We yelled, Dad rushed into the room, threw Ada to the floor, and rolled her up in the fireside rug. It was all over in a moment, Ada was quite unharmed, but we were all rather upset. Ada was most upset at the loss of her dress. Dad was upset by Ada's attempt to be some sort of fireworks display, and possibly set fire to the house. Mum was upset when she realised that any thought of going to the theater was out of the question, and Grandma Mary was upset because Elizabeth and I were keen for Ada to do it again.

Ada, wearing one of Mum's dresses, and Grandma left, and Elizabeth and I were put to bed. Mum and Dad cleared up the mess, so that the following morning there was little evidence of Ada's Roman Candle look-alike effort.

That might have been the first event that I remember.
The next was not quite so dramatic but I was never allowed to forget it.

Sister Elizabeth

Elizabeth had a rather super tricycle, which she seldom used, but which I envied more than anything. My tricycle was a very inferior thing, suitable only for indoor use. Elizabeth could race around outside, her tricycle being capable of anything a modern 4X4 sport utility vehicle can do. Around the house there were open concrete drains to carry rainwater from the gutter down-pipes away from the house.

My tricycle had small wheels, which dropped into these drains and stuck, necessitating dismounting, dragging the machine out and re-mounting. Elizabeth could ride over these drains as though they didn't exist. She also had a china-headed doll of which she was inordinately fond.

One day I saw Elizabeth's tricycle out in the garden, and decided to sneak a ride. Elizabeth saw me about to mount it, and decided that she must have a ride or her world would come to an end. She nudged me to one side, thrust her doll into my hands and rode off. I yelled to ask what I was now supposed to do, and she yelled that, if I wanted to ride, it would have to be on my own trike, which had a sort of flat platform to sit on instead of a saddle. I could straddle the doll on the tapered front part of the seat, and take the doll for a ride too. You may imagine what happened when I crashed into a concrete drain. The wretched doll toppled off, and smashed onto the drain, its head shattering into umpteen pieces.

Elizabeth looked back and let out a piercing scream. Mum rushed out of the house. I was scolded by both mother and sister for being a boy, being awkward, being clumsy, being impatient and being stupid.

The Passion Wagon

My experience at riding tricycles was to prove very valuable as I learned to steer, and became so expert that I was able to both steer and operate the pedals at the same time. My godfather, Matthew Armstrong, bought himself a

1932 model Morris Minor drop head coupe. This was a very small, smart car with which, I've no doubt, he hoped to lure pretty maidens to take rides into quiet places, where he could try to persuade them to do things that they wouldn't want photographed. Perhaps I credit him with a more lusty libido than was his due, but I can't think of any other reason why a young Scot would wish to equip himself with a 1932 Morris Minor drop head coupe.

Matthew came to our house to show off his passion wagon. My aunt, the beautiful, raven haired, Norah, was spending a day with us. Matthew, perhaps in an effort to impress Norah and show off his ability to get on with two-year-old boys, suggested I might like to go for a drive in the new car. Clearly no other member of my family was keen to risk life and limb, but I was eager. I sat on Matthew's lap so that, by craning my neck, I could see through the windshield and off we went, Matthew operating the pedals and gear lever, and I doing the tricky bit of steering.

We drove down the long path through the garden to 6th Ngong Avenue, a narrow, tree-lined lane. There we turned right and sped up hill to the T junction with the main highway where we turned around and drove back down 6th Ngong Ave. to the other end. We then returned home to be greeted as conquering heroes. Matthew was clearly amazed by my competence. We hadn't hit a single tree, pedestrian, cyclist or any other hazard, and this was deemed to be unusual for a two year old.

Had I been a few years older, I might have blown nonchalantly on my finger nails and polished them on my shirt breast in the age-old gesture of the cool champion. At the age of two, however, I was only able to show my pride by strutting around arrogantly. I was not to forget this adventure, and was not about to allow any member of my family to forget it either.

Matthew's lion

One day Matthew contacted Dad at his office. Matthew lived on the outskirts of Nairobi next what is now the Nairobi National Park. As is the case today, there was quite a large lion population in the area, and one night Matthew was awakened by a lion roaring in the garden. He looked out of the upstairs bedroom window and saw the lion immediately below him. Loading his shotgun with bird-shot, he aimed at the back of the lion's neck and fired. Even at a distance of about 10 feet, the bird-shot was not enough to kill the lion, which ran off. Realising how stupid he had been, and how he would face severe penalties if the Game Warden heard about the wounded lion, Matthew phoned to ask Dad to come out to try to follow the wounded lion into the scrub and dispatch it.

Dad was furious with Matthew for having been so silly as to shoot a lion with bird-shot. But he grabbed his rifle, and went off to see if he could find the lion to put it out of its misery. He followed a trail to the edge of a dry water course about fifty feet deep. The wounded beast was lying at the bottom of this *donga* (arroyo). As he saw the lion, he also saw a Masai tribesman on the far side of the donga, peering down at the lion.

Dad put a shot into the lion's brain, and the Masai, yelling for all he was worth, charged down the steep cliff, and hurled his spear. The spear passed through the lion and stuck into the hard ground. Dad felt he had to ensure the lion was really dead. He carefully and laboriously climbed down into the donga descending a cliff, the like of which the Masai had raced down at full speed. The Masai hacked off the end of the lion's tail, waved a cheery goodbye to Dad and left, proudly swinging the tuft of the lion's tail. He had blooded his spear on a lion, had proof of his deed and had earned his status as a warrior.

The Key

Another event was perhaps less dramatic but, for me, most traumatic. I had gone to the lavatory and was sitting on the throne, contemplating life, as chaps are wont to do. I had been told never to lock the door but, on seeing the big, shiny key in the lock, I decided that I was now old enough to have a go at operating the lock. I was quite amazed at how simple it was to turn the key, and was rather taken by the way the lock mechanism clicked so easily. I returned to squat on the loo and continued to consider the ways of the world.

In due course it was time to leave the loo, by which time I had forgotten that the door was locked. On being unable to open the door, a terrible panic overtook me. Even after realizing the problem, my flustered efforts to operate the key were fruitless. I hadn't undergone any training on lock operation, and was trying to turn the key in only one direction. The wrong one.

Bleats of terror rose to a crescendo of screams. Mum came to the door, calmed me, and explained how I was to remove the key and push it under the door. I thought for a moment that she might throw it away and leave me in the loo for the rest of my life, but I decided to trust her, and did as she instructed. A moment later I was released, and rushed past Mum into the freedom of the garden in the hope I might avoid a reprimand. In this I was surprisingly successful. Perhaps Mum thought I'd learned a lesson.

Later that day, when he returned home from work, Dad called me, took my hand, led me to the loo, and gave me excellent training in how to turn the key - one way to lock and the other way to unlock. I have never forgotten this training, and am able to approach almost any lock with the utmost confidence. Which just goes to show that even I can be trained by anyone with exceptional patience and understanding.

A Bloody WHAT????

Also about this time another big event involved the *shamba* boy. Gichau was his name. *Shamba* is a Kiswahili word meaning plot or garden, and boy is a corruption of an Indian word *bhai* (brother). In India, it seems, everyone is called *bhai* when their name or title is not known. Also, employees and servants may be called *bhai*. So, *shamba* boy or garden brother really means gardener. Gichau was our gardener.

One sunny day I heard Gichau singing in the garden as he went about his work. Singing seemed to be heard more often in those days. Anyway, I went out to see Gichau who was, up to that time, a good friend of mine. I found him pushing an empty wheelbarrow down the long drive to the bottom of the garden, where he had swept up heaps of leaves. With considerable arrogance I demanded a ride in the barrow. Gichau replied tersely that he was far too busy to play with an imperious, rude little boy, and walked off. So, I called him a bloody *pombafu* (uncivilised bastard). Gichau hesitated momentarily, and then walked on. Our friendship had snapped, and was only mended several years later.

That evening I saw my Dad talking to Gichau, who had affected a face as long as a boot. Shortly afterwards Dad came into the house, and found me quaking in a wardrobe from whence he took me, put me over his knee, and spanked me with his hand. Naturally, I screamed with all the vigor I could muster. Mum came running in, and Dad had to tell her why he had spanked me. When he told her what I'd called Gichau, she became angry, and demanded to know from whom I'd learned such words. She accused Dad of having sworn in front of the children - perfectly true.

My screams had been heard by Gichau who now seemed to feel remorseful for having snitched on me. So now four people were distressed: Me for having received corporal punishment, Dad for having been found guilty of using bad language in front of the children, Mum for having learned that Dad was guilty of irreparable damage to the kids, and Gichau for having brought about my spanking.

Father Christmas and the Ghillie-ghillie Man. (Itinerant Indian Magician).

After the loss of my friendship with Gichau, I made friends with Father Christmas. He was a small, thin Sikh gentleman with a long white beard who, once a week, came to the garden gate, pushing a large two wheeled hand cart full of fresh fruit of many kinds. On reaching the gate he would call out, and Mum would send the cook to buy bananas, mangoes, pawpaws (papayas), pineapples, oranges, avocados or whatever desirable fruit might be in season.

We called this very nice man Father Christmas because of his long white beard. On one occasion, when in my terrible twos, I had particularly displeased Mum, and she threatened to give me away to Father Christmas. So, the next time he came around, I decided to discuss with him the possibility that I might become his. Father Christmas, I discovered, did not speak much English, and my limited Kiswahili wasn't up to telling him that he might receive me as a gift, and that I thought him a very nice chap. He never fully understood the possibility that faced us.

However, my efforts were rewarded when he gave me a passion fruit, a particular favorite of mine, and we got along very well despite not being able to chat to each other. Thereafter, I took on the job of buying the fruit, the cook coming with me to carry my purchases into the house. I believe to this day that I made better deals with Father Christmas than any other member of our household, and I was very sorry when we moved into another house in an area that Father Christmas didn't visit.

I also remember a visit by a ghillie-ghillie man. He was an itinerant Indian magician who made small conifers grow up out from our front verandah wooden floor, did frightening things with spitting cobras which he had brought from India. These scared the socks off my Mum, scared my sister Elizabeth into her bedroom and left me, a two year old master negotiator, to haggle over the charge for his uninvited visit. Having argued for a considerable time, he wearily agreed to my offer, whereupon I had to get the money off Mum, who was hiding on the back verandah, and who asked me in an urgent whisper, "Has he gone?" I gave the money to the ghillie-ghillie man who went on his disconsolate way.

These are my earliest memories. I was still less than three years old when we moved in 1933 from Girouard Road to another house, which my Dad bought when he landed a new job with vastly better prospects. From the age of about twenty months to about thirty-two months, I had a number of experiences which had switched on my mental processes, and which I have remembered in detail all my life.

7

Growing up.

Dad's new job in Nairobi enabled him to buy a house on Sclater's Road, an arterial route leading westwards out of Nairobi. We lived there from 1933 to 1946, a period of my life which I much enjoyed, and during which I terrorized the neighbors and made some very good friends.

Greater affluence and more servants.

Having settled into the Sclaters Road House and explored it and its three acre garden, we decided that it was to be a wonderful, happy place for the family. New-found affluence enabled Dad to engage additional staff. Maina joined Gichau as a shamba-boy and Gitari joined us as house-boy. The succession of cooks now had an assistant who, while being called the kitchen-*toto* (child), was neither a child nor was he solely the cook's help as he also had to help Gitari with house work.

The house was a five bedroomed, 'dagga' built bungalow. The walls were about 18 inches thick of rough stones bound with a mud mortar, and rendered inside and out with a three-quarter thick cement plaster. The exterior of the walls was painted cream, the wooden window casements green and the corrugated iron roof was coated with red lead oil-bound paint. The fifth bedroom was an addition, and, like the other bedrooms, had its own wash basin. This bedroom became Dad's study and workshop, where I was later to spend many happy hours making, breaking, repairing and oiling things, including Mum's old, treasured, hand-powered Singer sewing machine.

Sewing Machine Repairman and Ovaltine

This particular repair caused Mum great distress as I hadn't informed her of my good deed, which was to be a wonderful surprise. A great surprise it was indeed. I had been too liberal with the oil, and when Mum began to sew up a dress that she had carefully cut out from expensive material, and had hand tacked together, the garment became drenched in dirty oil. My popularity waned but no action was taken against me as I had tried to be helpful, for a change. Anyway, the garment was only something Mum was making for Elizabeth, and so couldn't possibly have mattered to any great extent, in my opinion.

I was to become unwanted again when Mum became suspicious of brown stains on the wall under the dining-room window. Every evening Elizabeth and I were supposed to drink a cup of Ovaltine with our supper. I hated Ovaltine, which made me feel quite nauseous. But Mum insisted it was good for us, so when she left the dining-room, I toddled over to the window to pour out the Ovaltine. I was only about three, so was not tall enough to lean out across the 18 inch thick wall. The Ovaltine ran off the outer window ledge and down the wall. I was not aware of this nor of the brown stain it caused. Elizabeth, bless her, kept my secret.

One evening, when we were all strolling round the garden, Mum drew Dad's attention to the stains. Under interrogation by Dad - piercing look under a bright light, threats of stoppage of candy, etc., I did a George-Washington-like admission, and in a sweet voice, said "I cannot tell a lie. It was I." This piece of verse so stunned Mum that she grasped my hand rushed me into the house, and begged me to reiterate what I had just said, so that she had a record of my first poem. My crime went unpunished, and Ovaltine was withdrawn from the supper menu.

Clever lad - lessons learned

I took stock of my achievements, talents and skills, and was fairly satisfied now that I had reached the age of three, I could get much of what I wanted out of life by guile, and the underhanded manipulation of my parents and other adults. Elizabeth was occasionally a problem, but she was by now more and more shunning any contact with me, and this enabled me to be more successfully secretive as well as more cunning and sly.

In addition to these assets, I knew how to swear at the servants, extinguish an aunt if she burst into flames, operate locks, negotiate and bring off successful purchasing deals, gain the sympathy of adults when my father smacked me, and enrage Elizabeth. I felt satisfied, and looked forward with eager anticipation at the prospect of honing my skills and gaining more.

My third birthday was a disappointment. I had hoped that I might be given a racing bicycle or a Rolls Royce motor car, having proved my competence at driving Matthew's car, or a yacht or something nice. A day or two prior to my birthday, I'd started being helpful and pleasant to my parents and Elizabeth, all of whom regarded me with a jaundiced eye. But I kept on trying. Clearly I was unsuccessful as, whatever I was given, was highly forgettable. It was probably a new pair of shoes from Mum and Dad and a lollipop from Elizabeth. Grandma Mary, my aunts and uncle probably gave me nothing, saying they'd get me something for Christmas which was but a mere five days off. Birthdays too close to Christmas tend to be disappointing.

Elizabeth was, by the age of five, quite skilled at sewing, embroidery, knitting and was becoming competent at using Mum's hand-powered Singer sewing machine. Grandma Mary and Mum were wonderful needle women and seamstresses, so it was no surprise that Elizabeth showed expertise at such an early age. She made clothes for her teddy bear and dolls extraordinarily well, and decorated them beautifully with multi-colored embroidery. Elizabeth continued to improve her skills as she grew up.

Meanwhile, I too was learning, and had reasoned that by sharpening my skills in whining, wheedling, flattery and guile, I could get by pretty well. Hints led Uncle Jack to buy me a car. This was a tin toy made in Japan. Jack told me it was a Streamline, and for years I looked out, in vain, for this make on the roads. My toy had windows, a driver and passengers printed on it, and a clockwork motor. This soon ceased to function when it became clogged with grass, mud, bits of candy and other materials which seem to collect around small boys along with 'slugs and snails and puppy dogs' tails'

Crime and Punishment

It was about this time that I made my first and only foray into a life of serious crime. Where my sister was, I can't remember, but Mum took me with her when she went shopping. We went to a department store - Mum wanted an ironing board or some equally boring piece of household equipment, and we had to pass through the Toy Department.

Mum tried to hasten me through this area of the shop, but I had espied a very small toy cannon, which I simply had to have. Mum refused to buy it for me and hauled me on into the Housewares Dept. While she made her purchase, I couldn't stop thinking about the little cannon. I really wanted that cannon. As we left, I walked quietly behind Mum as we approached the Toy Dept, and looked around to see if there was anyone watching me. As we passed the cannon, I grabbed it, and put it in my pocket.

When we got home, I was stupid enough to play with my new acquisition on the lounge carpet, shooting bits of matchsticks at the settee. Mum was presumably out on the back verandah ironing, but she came into the lounge, and I was caught red-handed. My poor mother was devastated. She held her head in her hands. Her worst fear was becoming a reality. Her wretched, unwanted but much beloved son, had turned criminal. I stood dejectedly with the evidence at my feet.

The cannon was taken from me, and was put on the mantelpiece, where it was to stay for all to see. Mum told me she would explain to all her numerous visitors why the toy was there, and how I had become a shoplifter. She told me that she'd have to tell Dad on his return home that evening, which she did, and I received a spanking. I took this chastisement without my usual screams. I probably deemed it to be warranted.

The cannon stayed on the mantelpiece for some weeks, but as far as I know, nobody ever asked about it. As long as it was up there, it was a dark gray cloud which loomed over me. Finally, I managed to get a dining room chair, climb up on it, and grab the now hated toy. I returned the chair, and threw the cannon into the trash bin. The disappearance was never mentioned by my parents who, I suspect, had forgotten all about the cannon, and never missed it. I don't suppose that the shop's annual accounts showed the loss but, for me, the incident has never been forgotten, and I have avoided the temptations of shoplifting ever since. And so it goes......A propensity to criminal activities can be quashed early in life by a sound tanning and an extended sense of guilt.

My new territory

The Sclaters Road House was proving to be a happy place, and the garden was, for me, a wonderful space. The property had been a tennis club and, besides the five bedroomed main house, there was a three bedroomed guest house with an outside bath-house and separate loo. There were two garages, one for two cars and the other with a six car capacity, a tennis court and servants quarters. All this stood on a three acre plot with lawns, trees, flower beds, vegetable patch, masses of fruit trees, scented plants and climbable trees. There were plenty of places to hide, lawns to run about on, paths to run down and secret places from which to observe the antics of my family, our servants and neighbors.

Meet my new pal

As I reached the age of four, it was decided that a responsibility might induce me to be less feckless. During the night before my birthday, I was awakened by strange whines and yaps, apparently coming from the direction of the bathroom. I called out, and Mum came into my bedroom to allay my qualms, suggesting that I'd had a bad dream. I soon fell asleep and awakened again, shortly after dawn, when Mum, Dad and Elizabeth came to wish me a happy birthday.

I had overlooked the approach of this important anniversary, and was jolted out of my sleep with gleeful anticipation. I sat up in bed and was about to ask, "So, what have you bought me?" when I saw Dad was carrying a wickerwork hamper from which the sounds of frantic scratchings indicated that some animal was eager to get out.

Dad put the hamper on my bed and opened the lid. I peered inside and came face to face with a small puppy. I was overwhelmed by joy, and the puppy seemed delighted to see me. I looked up into the smiling faces of my family and gasped "Oh, thanks!"

I reached into the hamper and lifted the puppy out onto my bed. He thanked me by enthusiastically wagging his stumpy tail and peeing on my blankets. He was a short-haired fox-terrier, white with black patches, one of which was almost a perfectly four inch circular spot on his left side, and another about an inch in diameter to the right side of the root of his tail. His little ears were black, and the tips always flopped forwards. He had black socks on all four paws.

While Mum attended to the little wet problem, I took my new companion out into the garden where we ran about showing each other all the interesting places which we were later to explore at leisure. I was still in my pajamas, unwashed and in a state of high excitement, when Mum insisted that we come inside for breakfast. With considerable impatience, I hurriedly carried out my ablutions, dressed, and gulped down a few mouthfuls of fruit and cereal. As I asked for permission to get down from the table, I swung off my chair to take my new pal into the garden again.

"Not so fast," said Dad. "Come with me to the back verandah."

"But Dad," I cried impatiently, "I think he wants to pee again." I scooped up the puppy and headed for the door.

"Whoa! Don't rush off." Dad was insistent. "What are you going to call him? He must have a name."

"Huh?"

"You see. You haven't even given him a name."

"Huh?"

"Come on, son. You and I are going to have to have a chat. You have to know how to look after your new pet.

You have to think of a name for him. You have to learn to powder him to keep him free of fleas. You have to know where he is to be fed and what food to give him. There's a lot to learn."

Dad led the way to the back verandah, and began to teach me how to take care of my little dog. I listened attentively as Dad showed me how to attach a leash to the collar, brush the puppy, how to sprinkle Pulvex insecticide powder onto his back, and rub it into his short coat. He showed me his bowls, one for food and the other for water.

"Have you thought of a name for him yet?" asked Dad. I hadn't, so Dad suggested "Joe." The little dog looked up at him and wagged his tail in eager anticipation.

"That's his name," I cried excitedly. "That's his name. He knows his name. Dad, he already knows his name." Dad smiled down at me.

"Perhaps that is the name he was given at the kennels where we bought him. Put on his leash and take him for a walk. But remember he is only a puppy and may want to have a sleep again soon."

Joe and I went for a run down to the end of the garden, and returned to my bedroom where we both curled up on my bed to snooze, and recover from the excitement of the morning.

Joe became my constant companion. We spent days together and shared my bed at night. I left him only when Mum took me shopping, to the dentist or some other appointment. Joe was always happy when I returned, and I was always delighted by his eager greeting.

One day Joe kept me busy playing hide-and-seek. He wasn't very good at the game as he was too impatient to stay hidden, and came looking for me, little black eyes shining with glee, rear end and stumpy tail wiggling, and his mouth gaping and pink tongue lolling. If I ran away to hide, he immediately raced after me and, with the same body language, he told me that he was far better than I at the game.

The day was hot, and the sun shone down from a cloudless sky. Joe and I were soon sweltering. I threw myself down on the cool grass beneath a papaw tree. After he had given my face a liquid lick, Joe lay beside me panting happily.

I looked up through the leaves of the papaw tree, and saw a sight that took my breath away. Hundreds of big white birds were slowly gliding across the heavens, all in the same direction. They were very high, and had it not been for the leaves shading my eyes and helping me to focus, I would never have seen them. I watched them for a long time. Only occasionally did any of them flap their wings, and then it was only two or three beats. They seemed to drift effortlessly through the sunlit firmament on some peaceful mission.

Joe was disinterested when I tried to show him wave after wave of the wonderful procession. He thought I was drawing attention to the tree, so he got up and went over to pee on its trunk.

I suddenly felt compelled to share the experience, and rushed to the house to call Mum. Breathlessly I urged her to come out to see the fly-past, but she was reluctant to lie in the grass and look up through the papaw tree leaves. What would the neighbors think if they saw her lying on her back in the grass alongside her son and his puppy, staring up at the leaves of a papaw tree? But, unless she did this, she wouldn't be able to focus on the spectacle high in the blazing sky.

To my great disappointment, neither Joe nor Mum ever shared with me the miracle in the heavens.

8

An intrusion - Margaret.

There was a flurry of activity, the reason for which I was unaware. Grandma Mary came to our house to look after Elizabeth and me while Mum disappeared. Then there were all sorts of upheavals when Dad failed to return home after work. Grandma Mary seemed to be very worried after she received a phone call. Dad had been involved in a road accident, and was in the same hospital as Mum. What was Mum doing in hospital anyway? Why hadn't I been informed? Nobody ever told me anything. Elizabeth, at age seven, apparently knew more that I, but she wasn't talking, and Grandma Mary was too distracted to answer my questions. I shrugged and went to look for Joe. Perhaps he knew something. At least he would wag his stumpy tail when I spoke to him.

Then all sorts of excitement erupted. Aunts Norah and Ada suddenly arrived, and with Grandma Mary were all rushing about, but were too busy to explain what was going on. Elizabeth was still keeping tight-lipped. I sat for a few minutes in the lounge wondering why I was being kept in the dark. I decided to have a word with Joe, but as I got to my feet everyone rushed to the front veranda as a car, driven by Uncle Jack, rolled up to the front of the house. Out got Mum nursing something wrapped up in a shawl, and my aunts rushed down the steps to meet her. As Uncle Jack brought in luggage, the rest of the unruly mob gathered in the lounge. Mum sat down and Grandma Mary took my hand and drew me over to Mum.

"There, look, you have a little sister." I looked. The thing was apparently asleep, showing absolutely no interest in me, her older brother.

Everyone was bending over cooing at the thing. It occurred to me that this was a waste of time as it was fast asleep. I found the whole situation a complete bore, so I went to look for Joe. He was always full of life and loved to retrieve the old tennis ball I threw for him.

Dad arrived home the following day with his head bandaged. He, at least, was prepared to tell me what had happened. He had been driving along a quiet road when a sports car, driven very fast, crashed into the side of his car from a fork in the road. Dad's car had no doors, only cut-aways, and his car was knocked from under him so that he landed on the hood of the sports car. Stunned, Dad rolled forward onto the broken glass covered road, and a shard cut into his forehead, down across his eyelid and into his cheek. The wound bled copiously.

"Oooo, can I see?" I asked reaching up to try to lift the bottom edge of the bandage so as to take a look. Dad drew back and Elizabeth slapped my wrist, knocking my hand away.

"Leave Dad alone! Can't you see he's been hurt?" Elizabeth sighed mightily at the stupidity of boys in general and me in particular. I sauntered off to have a word with Joe. I wondered if he and I could find a safari of ants from which we could select a few big soldier ants to stitch up Dad's wound, but we found none. Wrong time of year for safari ants, we agreed. Things soon returned to normal -

almost. Aunts, Uncle Jack and Grandma left after more nauseating cooing, and after a few days Dad's bandage was removed to reveal a healing wound which had apparently been stitched by the doctor. I wondered if he had used soldier ants.

I remained unimpressed by my new sister, who spent a lot of time sleeping or crying. Mum kept disappearing into a bedroom, now referred to as the nursery, and when she came out, the baby had to be burped. This seemed to me to be an odd ritual. And there were times when there were unpleasant odors rising from the baby.

Altogether, I could see nothing to celebrate. The child was far too young for me to play with. It should have been born at about the age of four. It couldn't speak. It took up a lot of Mum's time, and it was about the only topic of conversation when visitors came to coo and croon over it. Joe and I ignored the little squirt.

I did have a hand in naming the brat. Our family was having a discussion about the only thing that seemed to be of interest to everyone except Joe and me. A number of names were suggested: Ann; Mary; Maud; Leonie; Frances; Rosemary; Alexandra...

"Margaret." The name burst from my lips

"That's it," said Mum and Dad together. I glowed with smugness, and for an instant my parents thought that my attitude towards my new sibling had changed. I sauntered out, hands in pockets, to tell Joe that I had chosen a name for the squaller. I left the choice of a second name to Mum and Dad. Disaster! Louise. What a ghastly name! Any interest in the infant that might have been stirring in my breast was squelched.

Formal education is on the horizon

As I approached the age of five, life was good but unpleasantness loomed. Elizabeth had started school - well

70

kindergarten actually, so I was without a playmate - Joan being off limits, Margaret being far too young, and Joe still a bit young to play all day. Not that Elizabeth was an entirely suitable playmate. Sisters never are, but she was better than nothing, and could at least be teased and enraged.

If Mum went shopping, she insisted that I accompany her. This was a bore as I had to sit alone in the car. To relieve the monotony, I practiced operating the steering wheel, the pedals, the gear shift, the windshield wiper controls, the windshield opening handle and the light switches. On one occasion I managed to release the parking brake, and the car slowly rolled forward into a shallow ditch. No damage was done, but Mum was a bit chagrined, and the incident led to the realization of my worst fears. I was sent to the school - kindergarten actually - which Elizabeth was attending.

I had absolutely no academic skills, and after Dad had introduced me to the head mistress, I was on my own, Elizabeth proving to be totally useless in helping me. She had run off to play with her friends disclaiming all knowledge of me. I was shepherded by a teacher into a playroom where we played with some toys, and later taken into the school grounds to play in a sand pit. I didn't mind this, but could see that I was going to have trouble with some of my fellow students who had some reading and writing skills. But before anything too drastic occurred, we were ushered into a classroom, and we had to start to learn to write. We were issued with ruled paper, and had to copy capital letters which had been written up on the chalk board.

Fairly quickly, I got the hang of doing the letter A and was put onto B. This proved too difficult, and the teacher was horrified when she realised that I was holding the pencil in my left hand. She immediately tried to rectify this aberration, which only made things more difficult for me. There was much argument and a flood of tears. By the time the teacher had dried her eyes, it was time for the lunch break, and I decided I'd had enough schooling and walked home, which was less than a mile away. There was some panic at the school when it was discovered I was missing. Elizabeth was questioned as to where I might be, but could only come up with statements that she hoped I'd left the country or had been eaten by wild animals.

Eventually, Mum found me on her return from a happy shopping trip, during which she hadn't had to worry that I was breaking her car. Naturally, I had to face the wrath of my Dad and a spanking, this time with his hair brush, to further impress upon me the seriousness of my offense. The headmistress determined that she and her staff were unwilling to have anything more to do with me, or my family - there had been words - and Elizabeth and I were sent to Miss Thomas's School several miles from our home.

Miss Thomas

Miss Thomas was a middle aged, stout lady who ran a school for brats from the age of about four to seven. She was skilled in the art of setting children on the path of the Three Rs. Unlike the first academy of learning to which I'd been sent, I was not expected to be able to read and write, and Miss Thomas sat me next to a very decent chap, Jeremy Watkins-Pitchford, the son of a doctor. Despite his lengthy name, Watkins-Pitchford was very understanding and sympathetic. He helped me considerably in the Three Rs, and more importantly, he made aeroplanes from Plasticine (modeling clay) for me. I could only manage balls and snakes. I watched W-P, and learned some manual skills.

Miss Thomas had an interesting speech defect. When enunciating the letter S, she whistled through her front teeth. The schoolroom had two rows of desks along the left wall where the youngest of us sat, two rows down the center for the next age group, and two rows down the right wall for the eldest kids, including Elizabeth. Miss Thomas had a desk with a telephone at the front, and from there she ran her world. Not just the teaching of about forty children, but the telephone enabled her to communicate with the outside world. When the phone rang, she would answer it saying "This is Miss Thomas's School. Miss Thomas, headmistress, speaking" and her problems with the alveolar fricative (sibilant letter S), sounded as though a flock of birds was passing overhead. This gave us much pleasure and caused great mirth.

I was ordered to take part in a school play. At the age of five I considered myself a big boy, and was reluctant to play-act, but I was persuaded that the role was an important one, not just a bit-part, but a leading, speaking interpretation. The play could not be produced without me, and the other players would not have the opportunity to tread the boards before the footlights, unless I agreed to take the role.

I and two other boys were to be ducks. Mum made up my costume consisting of a one-piece, white romper-suit with a hood to which was attached a yellow beak made from yellow velvet. A hole under the beak enabled me to see where I was going, and gauge the reactions of the audience. The holes where my feet stuck out were elasticized, and I wore duck's-feet-like yellow slippers, also made from velvet. Two quilted, shaped bags were attached to each side of the suit as wings, and a few paint strokes delineated eyes and feathers. Mum went to a lot of trouble.

I had to learn my lines and complicated choreo-graphy, and this took the best part of one full school term of three months. There were many rehearsals, but no full dress rehearsal, as it was thought that our elaborate costumes might get dirty. Finally the great day arrived. Parents filled the schoolroom chattering excitedly. The players hid backstage with a few parents who were organizing the production.

Stage fright overwhelmed me. I felt sure there was something I had forgotten, but I was called, and with two other ducks we walked on stage in single file with me

73

bringing up the rear. We spoke our lines as we circled back to leave the stage.

"Quack, quack, quack."

This elicited applause and remarks from the audience. "Oh! How sweet!" "Oh! How cute!" But no standing ovation. As a five-year-old big boy, I found the remarks rather sickening.

Adjacent to the schoolroom there was a hall and, having completed our appearance on stage, I rushed into this temporary changing-room, tearing off my costume. An awful premonition swept over me as I stepped out of the wretched romper-suit. Several girls were crowding round me.

"Just what do you think you're doing?" cried an irked mother/organizer, "You boys are supposed to go up to Miss Thomas's house to change." I suddenly realized that this was what had been nagging me before I went on stage. It was probably my worry that had detracted from my two minute performance, which had fallen short of a standing ovation.

I was now stark naked with a mob of girls peering at me. I hurried to get back into my costume, a difficult thing to do for a five-year-old boy, who had no experience as a quick-change artist. Then I ran up to Miss Thomas's house and thankfully got into my clothes.

Thus ended my career as a thespian.

***

Miss Thomas was an animal lover. In Kenya in those days, most kitchens were equipped with Dover stoves (wood burning ovens) and *kuni* (firewood) was delivered by ox-drawn, two wheeled carts. The ox drivers had long whips which they cracked an inch over the backs of the oxen. They did not actually touch the oxen, but it certainly appeared that they did, and the crack of the whip, and assumption that it was hitting the straining animals, was enough to make anyone wince.

One day a *kuni* delivery was being made, and the two oxen were hauling the heavily loaded cart up the steep school drive. The cart creaked under its one ton load, the whip cracked, and the ox drivers yelled to further urge on their poor emaciated beasts. The double doors of the schoolroom were wide open, and Miss Thomas looked out over our heads, and saw what appeared to be appalling cruelty being meted out by the ox drivers.

She rose to her feet, and dashed out of the schoolroom and down the drive, fists clenched, eyes red with rage, followed by forty excited children. The two ox drivers saw her coming, and were turned to stone. Miss Thomas snatched a whip and began, ineffectually, belaboring the two unfortunate drivers, who suddenly regained mobility, jumped off the cart, and took off at high speed down the drive and across the road. There they stopped to observe further events.

The oxen, now driverless but under the strain of the cart, were beginning to mill around, and the cart and oxen were in danger of rolling backwards, out of control down the steep hill. Miss Thomas was nonplussed, but realized that she was now responsible for a very serious situation. Fortunately my five year old friend, Billy Sands, knew what to do. He dashed to the rear of the cart, and putting his life in jeopardy, cranked the handle that screwed the mechanism that brought the brake blocks up against the wheels. He tightened the screw with all his might, and was joined by another kid who added his strength. The perilous situation was over. Miss Thomas stood panting with relief, and thanked God, Billy, and his chum. We all trooped back into the schoolroom, and the doors were closed. When lessons were over, we all went outside to find the cart gone. The wood had been off-loaded in the correct place, near the kitchen. The ox drivers had sneaked back and, with as little noise as possible, had finished delivering the *kuni*. Billy Sands was the hero of the day.

On to Muthaiga Day School

WHACK.....WHACK.....WHACK.....I felt the blood running down the back of my right thigh. I barely felt the next three whacks. My whole being was filled with hatred. I knew that the flogging was unfair. Mr Harsten, the headmaster of the Muthaiga Boys' Day School was beating us unjustly. He shoved me to one side and grabbed at my friend Mike Duggins, bent him over and delivered six whacks to his bare bum. Harsten, still raging, strode away to his office. A lady teacher escorted Mike and me to the toilet where she washed the blood away and applied zinc talcum powder liberally to our wounds.

I was six years old when I started at Muthaiga School for boys. I was barely seven and Mike was nearly eight when we suffered the thrashing. It had been worse for Mike as he had seen the blood running down from my flaying, and knew that he was to be flogged too. Neither of us cried. The feeling of injustice was paramount. I had felt the pain of the first three whacks. Then hatred had flooded through me, overshadowing any other emotions and feelings.

While our wounds were being treated, I remember being worried that the blood would soil my underpants and shorts, and that a worried Mum would ask questions. In a sense, I had the same unjustified feeling of guilt that rape victims are said to experience. Had we really been guilty of some heinous wickedness?

Why had we been beaten so brutally? Earlier that day at Assembly, Harsten, (I deny him the title of Mr. He was a criminal, and, as is customary under British Law, he loses all titles) had announced that we were to always wear our hats when going outside. In Kenya in those days (1930s) it was thought that it was dangerous for Europeans to venture out without a hat. Their brains would overheat and become addled.

The school uniform required us to wear double terrai hats. These were wide brimmed, felt hats with a double

76

crown. An alternative was the sola topee, a helmet made from sola reed pith to make an effective solar helmet. Sola reeds are found in India and the helmet is comparatively light. I wore one of these at home, but the helmets were not part of the school uniform, perhaps because they were hard and might be thrown, Frisbee-like, at teachers. Double terrais were rather heavy, and tended to fall off during highly active games such as cops and robbers.

During Assembly, Harsten had told us that there was a discussion going on in the local daily, the East African Standard, as to whether it was safe for Europeans to subject their bare heads to the sun in Kenya, which lies across the Equator. The editor of the newspaper was adamant. Europeans should not let their brains become addled. He was supported by members of the medical profession. Being only seven years of age, much of this discussion went over my head, and almost all of what Harsten had to say that day escaped me - and Mike, my best buddy at the time.

Consequently, two hours after he had given his dissertation on the subject of double terrais, Harsten spotted Mike and me tearing around the school grounds playing cops and robbers, hatless. Rage welled up, and he screamed at us - and the rest of the boys.

We gathered at the front door of the school. Mike and I stood on the top step behind Harsten, and the rest of the school formed a half circle below. Harsten had a favorite student, an Italian boy, Fabrizzio, of about eighteen years of age who was attending our school to improve his English.

Normally the school took boys up to the age of 13, although we did have one or two slow 14 year olds - their brains having been addled by the sun?

Harsten sent Fabrizzio to cut a cane from the clump of bamboo that grew in the school grounds. The wretched Fabrizzio returned a few minutes later, proudly carrying a 30 inch long, carefully selected cane. This he handed to Harsten who ordered Mike and me to remove our shorts and underpants. We then had to suffer the indignity of being whacked, bare bummed, in front of all the boys.

Although only seven years old, I know that if I'd had a pistol, I would have killed Harsten. Maybe our misdemeanor did warrant punishment, but not the thrashing Harsten meted out. I have long mulled over the effects of the beating. I cannot believe that the intense hatred that Harsten provoked was either normal or beneficial for small boys to experience. Nor can I understand why it was that Mike and I failed to tell our parents of the incident. It was, I think, due partly to our feeling of guilt, but also to a sort of weird question of honor. We were bound not to snitch on our school.

A few days later, I was brushing my teeth at the basin in the bathroom. Having just bathed, I was nude. Mum came in, looked at me, and went out again. Moments later Dad came in. He saw the wounds, now beginning to heal, wrapped a towel round me, and led me to my bedroom. We sat together on my bed with Dad's arm around my shoulders.

"What happened to you, son?" he asked gently.

The game was up. I had to confess. By degrees, Dad got the whole story out of me. He went to telephone Mike's Dad who questioned Mike. Our tales corroborated. I do not know what, if any, action our parents took. In those days it was commonly believed that, if a boy fell off a horse, it was best that he be put back in the saddle immediately.

Perhaps Mum and Dad had debated what should happen. Perhaps Dad thought that I had taken the punishment 'like a man', and maybe he was proud of his son for not having whined to his parents. Mum may have wanted to take me from the school immediately. But I hadn't missed a day, and had continued to go to school after the flogging without apparent reluctance. I suspect that the debate was hot, as the subject was never again mentioned. I was 'back in the saddle' and was seemingly unspoiled.

The best of my experiences at Muthaiga School were that Michael and I were both to become proficient in the art of boxing. We had a wonderful instructor, Bob Billings, who had been the British Army Heavyweight Boxing Champion in India in his day. He taught us to spar, not fight, and Mike and I were champions.

Mike was a year or so older than I, and beat all the older boys in the school. I too managed this, but I could never beat Mike, who was very much more skillful. I could jump more than my own height, and could run faster than Michael, but it was the sport of boxing which drew us together, and I was quite happy with our pecking order.

Mike was sent to England in 1938 to receive his education there, and was to become the lightweight amateur boxing champion of southern England as a young man.

During Michael's school days in England, the outbreak of WW II made travel difficult, and he was unable to visit Kenya. His parents were obliged to travel, by whatever means they could, to see their son. Mike was a boarder at school, and during school holidays, he stayed with relatives.

In addition to the normal school fees, Mr Duggins paid extra for boxing lessons. But Michael had come to hate boxing, and, at the beginning of one term, he told the headmaster that the extra money was for violin lessons. The headmaster took his word for this, although Mr. Duggins had stated the letter in which he enclosed his check, the fee for boxing lessons was included. Michael persuaded the headmaster that his Dad, in a moment of absentmindedness, had written boxing instead of violin lessons. So, Michael became a wannabe Yehudi Menuhin.

Towards the end of that term, Mr Duggins visited the school, and asked the headmaster how Michael's boxing was proceeding. Michael's 'fiddling' was discovered. So annoyed was Michael that he became a determined fighter, and thrashed anyone silly enough to get into the ring with him.

It was, perhaps, his fighting spirit that led him to join the Royal Air Force. He became a bomber pilot, and took part in the Berlin Airlift in 1948. After service in the RAF,

Michael became a sales representative for a fountain pen manufacturer. Tragically, he died as a young man in an auto smash.

Before my own leaving of Muthaiga Boys School, I experienced two other incidents during the remainder of the term after the beating. I had been feeling unwell, and had told Mum, who thought that I was reluctant to go to school because of the caning I had suffered. To school I had to go.

During the morning a lady teacher saw that I was pale and clearly unwell, and sent me to the sanitarium. This consisted of a wooden hut which had been built on the flat roof over part of the ground floor of the building. The flat roof had a three foot high stone parapet along one side.

There was another boy in one of the two beds. He was covered in perspiration and shaking with fever. I was put into the other bed, and my mother was phoned.

Harsten came to the sanitarium, and asked why the fevered boy was there, which was pretty obvious. Malaria was common in those days. He asked what the boy's temperature was, and was told the lad had bitten the thermometer in his ague. Assuming the boy had deliberately broken it, Harsten, in his madness, grabbed the boy by the arm, dragged him to the parapet, and he threw him over onto the paving below. Fortunately the semi-conscious boy landed feet first, and suffered only a cracked ankle.

Later, Harsten's wife committed suicide after killing their son. Harsten ended up at a nursing home where I saw him many years later, a barely recognizable, morose, emaciated, wizened figure without a friend in the world. I had no sympathy for the man.

The feelings of sickness which caused me to go to the dispensary were to lead to having my appendix removed. It was found, after a long search, tucked in the back instead of near the front of my tummy. The operation required an 11 inch incision, which, on a boy of seven, is a mighty long one.

The offending appendix was in a poor state due, the doctor said, to passion fruit, guava and tomato seeds getting lodged in the end of the large intestine and festering. Maybe my old friend, Father Christmas, had had his revenge for my having beaten his prices for fruit down to sub-economic levels.

The obligatory ten days were spent in hospital, and then another week of recuperation at home, where I experienced the warmth of my family. The affection Dad had shown when he saw the injuries caused by the caning I had received from Harsten, was not unusual. Sometimes in the evenings, after Elizabeth and I were ready for bed, having bathed and eaten our supper, Dad would have us sit on the wide arm rests of his chair. He would put his arms around us and ask us what we had been doing that day. These moments were warm and comforting. I don't remember Mum ever doing the same sort of thing but, never-the-less, we knew she loved us more than life itself.

9

Mum doesn't learn to play golf

Dad's tendency to become a bit impatient was evident again some years after his honeymoon show of temper. Dad had been a good sportsman, particularly at swimming and tennis. But a few years of married life to a champion housewife, whose greatest pleasure was to get into the kitchen, and make superb, high calorie tarts, pies and other pastries, had resulted in an increase in dad's girth. Such games as tennis were no longer attractive to him.

Mum had never been a sportswoman. She shunned all forms of sporting exertion, being content to cook, make all our clothes, make rugs and beautiful tapestries, knit socks, jumpers, cardigans and embroider my sister's frocks and blouses. In addition to these activities she loved to read, and she devoured books at an enormous rate. She ran a super-efficient house. and looked after her progeny, keeping them clean, bright and shiny most of the time. One day Dad came home and announced that he had been thinking. Mum feigned interest.

"Golf," announced Dad, "that's what we should take up. It's a game we can both play, and one that we can enjoy together. Imagine it! You and I could start off early on a Sunday morning, and enjoy a quiet amble round the golf course. We'd both benefit. We both need a bit of exercise, and it's a simple game to play. After all, the golf ball is stationary. It just sits there waiting to be hit. As someone has said, you put one small ball down on a very big one and try to hit the small ball without hitting the big one!"

Dad chuckled, trying to enthuse Mum, but she was concentrating on a particularly complicated part of a knitting pattern. Dad waxed lyrical in an effort to sell Mum his brilliant idea. He ended by saying "I'll take a few lessons from a pro and, when I'm reasonably competent, I'll teach you, and you can practice during the week. It'll give you something to do. It'll be fun!" Dad seemed not to notice mum's continued silence.

Dad had a few lessons, and became over-confident as all beginners do. Mum received a set of golf clubs in a handsome bag for her birthday. For her, the present was about as welcome as a dead toad. That very evening Dad gave her the first golf lesson. He showed amazing patience.

"This is the way to grip the club . This is the way to address the ball. This is the way to take the club back, keeping the left arm straight. This is the correct position when at the top of the back swing. Now we start the downswing. This is the position to be in as we hit the ball. Notice my head is down making sure that contact is made with the ball. And this is the way we follow through with the right heel lifting as we swing our hips for a full finishing turn."

Mum took a swipe at the ball and missed.

"Don't worry," said Dad gently. "Even I missed the ball when I started. Now, watch me again. This is how we start the back swing."

Mum took another swipe and missed.

"Try again, darling," said Dad patiently. Mum took another swipe, and knocked the ball two feet off the tee. She bent down, grabbed the ball, placed it on the tee and smashed it into the middle of next week.

"There you are!" exclaimed Dad proudly, as though it was he who had performed a near perfect shot.

"You'll soon get the knack. All you have to do is practice each day. After all, you have nothing else to do, and if you put in, say, seven hours a day, you'll soon be better than me!"

Regrettably, Mum was very busy during the next week making mince pies for Christmas, darning my well worn socks, and winding bandages for the hospital. She had no time to practice.

In his enthusiasm, Dad assumed that she had been practicing seven hours a day while he had been at work. He was a little disappointed when she had three air shots in succession, and he felt it necessary to go through the interminable routine of "This is how we start the back swing..............."

"Now," he wound up the lesson "You must practice. That's all it takes. And, after all, you have little or nothing to do all week."

Well, Mum did have rather a lot on her hands the following week, and was again unable to find the time, or enthusiasm, to practice. So the next lesson started with another three air shots and Dad's patience began to ooze away.

"I can't understand what the problem is. After all, you only have to hit a stationary ball. Give me that bloody club." He almost snatched the club from Mum, shouldering her out of the way. With great deliberation, he took a mighty swing.

He missed the ball. He threw the club across the garden and stormed off shouting, "Is this a game or a bloody disease?" So ended my parents' venture into golf.

Mum, the Firefighter

If Mum seemed out of her depth in sporting matters, she was extraordinarily practical in household affairs, and surprised us on at least one occasion. When I was about eight, I had been given a toy steam engine consisting of a boiler mounted on a three-sided metal box which served as a housing for a spirit burner. Attached to the boiler was a piston, fed with steam under pressure from the boiler. The piston drove a flywheel. There was a safety valve on the boiler which was supposed to be set so that the head of steam pressure was limited by the safety valve releasing excess pressure. But I discovered if the safety valve was screwed down, the piston drove the flywheel round at a tremendous speed.

In the interests of science and engineering, I screwed the safety valve down tight. The engine went berserk. The flywheel spun at a rate that was fairly exciting, and I thought it prudent to release a bit of pressure. But everything was now hot, and, try as I might, I couldn't undo the safety valve which seemed to have jammed. The engine revs rose and the whole device started to shudder. The spirit burner tipped over spreading burning spirit over the floor. Now my in-depth study of things scientific and engineering had gotten out of hand, and the wooden floor of the veranda was burning merrily.

I screamed. Mum rushed out onto the veranda. In a split second she saw what was happening. She dived back into the house, and reappeared with a cigarette ashtray of sand and a broom. She threw the sand into the flames and then calmly brushed the sand, with the flames, off the verandah, down the stone steps and into the garden. End of inferno!

I was mightily impressed with Mum's calm, rapid solution to the problem. I was very proud of her, and I suppose I showed it in some way.

10

A succession of schools

At the Muthaiga School for Boys, I had begun to learn to read and write a bit more, and came up with correct answers in arithmetic more frequently. My left-handed writing was appalling. We wrote in ink using sharp pen nibs with split points, dipping the nib into an inkwell set in a hole on the right hand top edge of each desk. Being left-handed, I had to push the pen across the paper. One side of a sharp nib point caught in the paper and then flicked out, spraying ink over the page. After dipping the pen in ink, I had to take it across the page, and blobs of ink dripped onto the paper. My copy book looked as though a spider with inky feet had walked across it.

Teachers constantly tried to get me to write right handed. This, together with the additional problem of having to copy, at the age of six, a Latin vocabulary, only exacerbated my misery, and the ghastly mess I made when writing. We started learning Latin at the age of seven in our first year at Muthaiga School. Harsten taught this subject, and on one occasion had to leave the classroom as we laboriously copied Latin words in our books.

"When I return," he warned, "all want to hear is the scratching of pens on paper." My bet is that he certainly heard my pen stridently rasping its way across the ink splattered page.

Another problem for left-handed writers is that their hand smears what they have just written. Many left-handers end up writing upside down, and I tried this with some success. But my elementary hieroglyphics continued to be a dreary problem for me, and my teachers. I hated writing.

St Andrews School

I left Muthaiga Boys' School at the end of the term, all my school uniform, including the too-heavy double terrai hat, becoming redundant. After experiencing Harsten's madness, I was happy to join Elizabeth, as a boarder, at St. Andrews School, Turi on the western side of the Great Rift Valley, pending my entry to Kenton College. Elizabeth was very happy at her school, and I looked forward to my short sojourn there. The school was owned and run by Mr. and Mrs. Lavers, who were very popular, and concentrated on a wide range of activities. We didn't box, but we did all sorts of athletics, carpentry, nature study, and went for long educational walks through beautiful farms.

I was particularly fortunate in that one of the teachers was an elderly man who had taught me at Muthaiga Boys' School. He was aware of the unjust beating I'd received, and my attempt to keep it a secret for the honor of the school. He and I were 'new boys' at St. Andrews together, and Scotty and I kept a friendly eye open for each other. Under his coaching, I won virtually every race which I entered at the end-of-term athletics meeting, and walked off with half a dozen first prizes in the form of fountain pens.

Scientific Experiments

I was almost five years older than Margaret. I started at boarding school when I was seven, leaving my two-year-old sister, and for the next seven years saw little of her. By the time I became a day scholar at the age of thirteen, Margaret was attending boarding school. Then I went to university in Dublin, and when I returned home, Margaret was about to go to London to become a nurse.

Perhaps it was a good thing that we spent so little time together. During one school holiday when I was about ten and Margaret five, I decided to carry out an in-depth scientific study into ejection seats. I had heard about these mechanisms, and the lives they had saved when fighter aircraft went down in flames. I grabbed Margaret, and ignoring her protests, dragged her to the site of my intended empirical experiment. This was a garden bed, fairly recently dug over. I lay on my back on the grass lawn with knees drawn up to my chest, my feet towards the garden bed. I instructed Margaret to sit on the soles of my feet and, when she was more or less ready, I straightened my legs with all the vigor I could muster. Margaret took off in an almost perfect trajectory, describing a beautiful arc.

Unfortunately, as her trajectory changed, so did her angle of approach, and she plunged nose first towards the soft earth with her little arms outstretched to limit facial damage. There was, in my opinion, no need for the change she had made in her angle of approach. I never got to the bottom of her ill-starred decision. She had left the launching pad in the shape of one sitting in a comfortable armchair. There was absolutely no reason to change this. By adopting a nose first flight, she jeopardized the whole experiment.

The garden bed was soft, but not that soft. She crash-landed and screamed. She struggled to her feet, and nursing her left arm, ran sobbing into the house. I followed more slowly, and tried to explain to Mum how Margaret had brought her injury on to herself. I accompanied my explanation with a graceful arcing movement of my arm, but Mum ignored my rationale and informed me that I was an unthinking, inconsiderate jackass. Margaret was only a girl, and she was too young to play with a ruffian. Dad would deal with me on his return from work. He did, by an assault with a hairbrush on my posterior.

A few months later, I was to engage in another scientific test. I was very interested in saving the lives of airmen who had to jump from crashing airplanes. When Mum went out to do some shopping, I decided to look into parachute design. I found a large brown paper bag, and with some difficulty attached, around the open end, looped threads. The paper was flimsy, and tore as soon as I tightened the loops, so I thought it prudent to use five instead of four lines, and to leave the loops loose. I was to jump off the roof of an outside wash house into a strawberry bed. A tree provided access to the roof, somehow, by the time I had gained my drop-off point, two of the five threads had torn from the paper bag. Further delay might be catastrophic as a breeze was tugging at the bag. I hastened to jump. As I accelerated through the twelve foot drop, the paper bag tore loose, and I was left with five lengths of thread in my hand, and a paper bag floating uselessly down behind me.

I hit the strawberry bed quite hard. The earth was soft but not that soft, and I was shaken. Elizabeth, now fourteen, on hand in case of injuries - she had decided to be a nurse at the age of four - helped me to a patch of grass where I sat wondering whether it was really worthwhile carrying out further scientific tests.

"What have you done to your ankle?" asked Elizabeth. I looked down and saw my anklebone exposed through an inch long cut.

"You'd better let me cover that up. It looks ghastly." I silently agreed, but found that I was completely unable to get to my feet. So I crawled on hands and knees 150 feet to the house, with an excited Joe leaping around, delighted with

the new game in which I was acting like a dog, at more or less his level.

On reaching the house, Elizabeth insisted, against my most emphatic disapproval, on washing the exposed bone with a wet face cloth to remove bits of strawberry bed. She then applied zinc powder, and covered the wound with a piece of lint held in place by a tight bandage. When Mum returned home, she demanded to see the injury, but the lint was firmly stuck. With copious amounts of water and despite cries of anguish from me, Mum managed to free the lint from the bone. She applied zinc oxide cream, drew the sides of the wound together, and stuck a strip of sticking plaster across, to stop bits of me falling out through the cut.

Elizabeth, in the interest of medical science, had revisited the site of my free-fall, and had found a piece of a glass bottle in the not-so-soft earth. We assumed that it was this that had cut my ankle. My family were in unanimous agreement that I had brought about the injury by my own stupidity. I discussed the incident with Joe whose demeanor suggested that he was in favor of ignoring their judgment. After a few days, Joe and I were again racing around the garden, Joe maintaining that activity hastened recovery.

Kenton College

Again, I was fitted out with a school uniform. This time the theme color was blue on a gray background, and this time, besides a smart blue blazer, I had a pair of dark gray flannel slacks - which I only wore once, in the fitting room on the day they were bought.

Kenton College was owned and managed by Mr. David Cramb, a Scot with a background of athletic achievement, having represented Scotland at pole vaulting and field hockey, and being expert in shinty, an extremely dangerous form of field hockey that only the Scots are crazy enough to play. He chose the snooty term 'College' which he thought appropriate to the inflated level of school fees he charged. Mum undoubtedly liked the snooty name, and thought it an appropriate academy for her son to attend.

Mr. Cramb had lost an eye when playing rounders, a form of soft-ball that British children play. The tragic event occurred when a short sighted teacher made up the numbers for one team and Mr Cramb joined the other team. The myopic master was not expected to make contact with the ball, and Mr. Cramb, who was pitcher, lobbed a slow ball which the master hit right in the middle with full force. The heavy, wet ball hit Mr. Cramb, knocking his eye permanently out of action. Forevermore he regarded us out of his good eye, always, it seemed, with deep suspicion.

But Mr. Cramb rarely caught any of us committing high crimes and misdemeanors, because of his habit of jingling his money in his pocket. We could hear his approach, and had plenty of time to put away the roulette wheel, cards, cigarettes, and bottles of gin before he reached us.

A map was prepared by one of the masters, Jack Hastings, who was our geography teacher. The map showed Eastern Africa and we were able to follow the war in Abyssinia (Ethiopia), Italian Somaliland and Eritrea (Somalia).

The war went well for the Brits as many of the Italians were decidedly against it and surrendered in droves. On one occasion, over 100 Italian soldiers surrendered to one British officer and a sergeant. The were happy to be out of the hostilities, although they would now be prisoners.

Hey! Mr Hitler

It was about this time that I went to war against Hitler. I was eight years old when war broke out on 3 Sept, 1939. Dad had been given a most embarrassing job. There was a fairly large, well respected Jewish community in

Nairobi, and many of them were German Jews. It may have been thought that German Nazi Party Members, masquerading as German Jews, had infiltrated into that community. Dad had a number of friends in the Jewish community. Several were successful businessmen, two running hotels, one ran a transport company, one a furniture manufacturing company. Others were farmers and coffee planters, doctors and lawyers. They were honorable folk whose handshake was as good as, or better than, any written contract.

So, Dad was very uncomfortable when he was asked to go and collect a number of German Jewish families, and take them to a police station for screening. Each person was allowed to bring one small suitcase. They had been warned that they were to be picked up, and were to be ready.

Dad was required to be armed, and this in particular he found galling. He was issued with a British army .303 rifle and a bayonet, presumably to hasten the reluctant and the recalcitrant into the car.

Dad had a 1932 Chevrolet sedan. There was no trunk, but it had a folding metal grill at the rear. This folded down for baggage to be strapped on it. So, the collection of each Jewish family was to take a few minutes.

In order to dilute the embarrassment of the occasion, Dad took me along with him. I sat beside him with the rifle, bayonet fixed, upright between my knees. Had Hitler known who his armed adversary was, he'd have surrendered without further ado. Dad needn't have worried, as the Jews were taking the whole procedure in the best of spirits, and were sensitive to the embarrassment that Dad was feeling. Dad would draw up at the front of a house, and out would come the family, each member carrying a small suitcase.

"Ah! Harold. How are you? What a how-do-you-do! Where do we put these?" Dad would stack the cases on the grill and tighten the straps. Then everyone would pile into the car. "And this is your son? What a fine boy he is. How old is he? What does he want to study? He looks such an intelligent boy." Little did they know the rascal they found so winsome.

On arrival at the police station, they collected their belongings, and thanked Dad saying "You must come for a meal, and bring your lovely wife."

They merged with the other members of their community waiting to be processed by policemen, who had little idea as to what they were supposed to do other than to ensure that each German Jew had friends or relations to support their claim to be genuine members of the German Jewish congregation. After providing their names, addresses, details of the number in their family and their ages, details of their occupations and other basic information, they were allowed to return home. It was a time consuming, tedious process, much of it repetition of previous bureaucratic interviews held at the time they entered the Colony, but it was taken with outward good humor. And so ended my first day of war against that madman, Hitler.

I suspect that none of the Jews was detained. Why should they be? Possibly they were told to be circumspect when writing to friends and relatives in Europe, as it is too easy to accidentally provide information that the enemy can use.

Blevets

Typically, the Brits were ill prepared for WW II. In Abyssinia (Ethiopia), they used their flair for 'making do' with what was available. They had no bombs - or bombers for that matter, and so the 'blevet' was born. This was twelve pounds of human excrement in a brown paper bag, and was dropped from low flying light airplanes. Or so it was said. One imagines that soldiers with low morale might well surrender swiftly when 'blevets' rained down after being shredded by the prop-wash. No doubt the question "Where were you when the sh*t hit the fan?" was first asked by a disgusted Italian officer as he flicked bits off his no-longer impeccable uniform.

Many of the Kenya conscripted soldiers drove their own cars up to fight in Abyssinia, and many preferred their own rifles to the antiquated, worn out Lee Enfield .303 rifles with which they were issued.

At school we sang lustily, a popular song of the time-

There's a war in Abyssinia, won't you come?
Bring your own ammunition and your gun.
Mussolini will be there, shooting pea-nuts in the air.
There's a war in Abyssinia, won't you come.

While the campaign had the reputation of being a rather amateur affair, there was some heavy fighting against determined, well trained Italian soldiers from northern Italy. A Kenya Regiment sergeant of the famous Leakey family was posthumously awarded the Victoria Cross, Britain's highest award for gallantry. Sergeant Nigel Leakey attacked a squadron of enemy tanks. He climbed up to open the turrets and shoot the occupants with a revolver. His action encouraged the remaining tank crews to beat a tactical withdrawal. The Italians retreated northwards for over 2,000 miles. The Abyssinian Campaign, as it is officially named, was also known as the 2,000 Mile War.

At school we were elated by the successes of the Brits, as many of us had relatives fighting in the campaign. We chattered happily as news of the British advance northward, away from Kenya, poured in daily and the threat diminished. But not all the news was good.

My uncle, Jack Chambers, was a gunner and suffered blown eardrums. He and other wounded soldiers were sent back to Kenya in a convoy of 15 trucks, each truck having a female nurse.

Somewhere in the mountains on a narrow twisty road, they were ambushed by a gang of 'Shifta' Somali tribesmen. All the women were raped, and all the men were castrated. They were stripped of their clothing, and were freed to walk, bare foot, through the broiling sun to the next British camp. Not all survived the ordeal, and my uncle never spoke of it. He remained isolated from the world by his injuries, and never married. He lived quietly with his mother, my grandma Mary, until her death at the age of 86. He then went to live in Britain, alone and without the wonderfully cheery character that his mother always was. He never wrote to us, and we only learned of his death through lawyers. He left nothing but the painful memories of a loyal soldier and a reliable worker.

*

When the North African campaign started, Jack Hasting's map was to bring us far greater worry. Rommel's Afrika Korps in North Africa presented very different problems from those of the Italians in the Abyssinian Campaign. The battle front lurched wildly from east to west and back again, as the fortunes of war swung first one way and then the other. We watched the changes on the map with elation, followed by consternation when Rommel pushed the allies back, almost to Cairo.

Then came the big battles, and the push back westwards until the Germans were concentrated around Tunis. The Americans then came into the war, but initially suffered a severe trouncing by Rommel. Our elation when the Americans joined in, was turned to despair when their green troops and inexperienced commanding officers failed to prompt Rommel's immediate surrender. But soon the war in North Africa was over, and the allied landings in Sicily heralded the Italian campaign.

We heaved a sigh of relief that the enemy were out of Africa, and wished we could join the army, to fight with the 'Desert Rats' of the 8th Army, or the Royal Air Force to fly Spitfire fighters, or to join the Royal Navy to take part in the War in the Atlantic. But, much to our chagrin, the British services weren't interested in enlisting boys of eleven or twelve.

We met servicemen who had seen war in Africa, Italy or had endured the Blitz, when Britain stood alone against better equipped and trained German forces.

Mum and Dad frequently offered accommodation to servicemen when on leave, who otherwise had to live in temporary military cantonments. Among other servicemen, two Royal Navy sailors, Eric and 'Long', spent leaves with us, away from the hot, humid port of Mombasa. My meetings with servicemen gave me the opportunity to demand that they hand over military buttons and badges for my collection. I also heard more intimate details of battle experiences, the courage displayed, and terror inflicted by the horrors of war.

We were elated when Hitler attacked the Russians, and had two fronts on which to fight. I remember an occasion when I boarded a train with a school friend, Sammy Rifkin, to return to Nairobi after a short school holiday on farms. We were joined on the train by two burly Afrikaner farmers, who said that we were no doubt happy that the Russians were now our allies. "But you mark my words," said one of the Afrikaners, "those Ruskies are going to cause trouble for many years to come."

The Enemy at Our Door?

When the enemy in North Africa pushed the allied forces back towards Cairo, we wondered if we would have to flee southwards to South Africa? Would the enemy parachute in to capture Nairobi? Had spies infiltrated into our midst?

One night at about 7:30 p.m. my family was sitting in the lounge reading, when Joe let out a low growl. This was most unusual. We all sat up and listened intently. Were we about to be attacked by a crack force of enemy paratroopers? Fears of invasion arose again within us.

There was a creak from the veranda floor. Joe growled again. Another creak. Somebody was moving stealthily across the veranda, and we could hear the footsteps through the closed, curtained glass door that led from the lounge onto the veranda. Signaling for us to be quiet, Dad rose from his chair, and tiptoed across the lounge into the hall. There was another glass door leading from the hall out onto the veranda, which was lit by a lamp over the steps from the verandah that led down into the garden.

As he reached the door, Dad saw, through the obscured glass, the silhouettes of two people on the veranda. He reached for his heavy walking stick and, holding it like a rifle fitted with a bayonet, he wrenched the door open and lunged forward.

He jabbed Mrs. Riddout on her bony elbow.

There was embarrassment all round because the Riddouts were our next-door neighbors. It was clear that they had sneaked up onto our verandah with the intention of listening to our conversation. Dad's attack was, perhaps, not entirely justified. But there was a war on, and who was to know that the enemy hadn't arrived?

The visitors were invited in, and Mrs. Riddout insisted that her elbow was quite all right, but she kept rubbing it until Mum went to get the butter. A little was applied to the now swollen, discolored elbow. Mum assured the injured snooper that this cure would minimize the bruise and swelling. Butter on a bump was Mum's favorite remedy.

Mrs. Riddout, an extremely emaciated little woman. She often came over to our house to borrow a cup of sugar, but Mum was convinced that these visits were just to pry into Mum's activities.

Mrs. Riddout appeared to be dominated by her husband although, to us, he seemed a most amiable man. Every Sunday at precisely 9:00 a.m. she could be seen taking a boiled egg in an egg cup out to her husband who sat at a table on the veranda. Mr. Riddout carefully cracked the shell with a teaspoon, removed the top and shook a liberal amount of pepper onto his egg. A moment later he sneezed, violently. His sneeze could be heard throughout the valley. People would smile in the comfortable knowledge that it was Sunday, 9:00 a.m., and that all was right with the world. Mr. Riddout had had his Sunday morning sneeze.

Mr. Riddout was Nairobi's Town Clerk, a senior financial executive's job that many might suppose would have been carried out by a serious, lugubrious pedant. But Mr Riddout was a very popular, unusually outgoing, Kenya character with a great sense of humor. He was also the target of a life insurance salesmen, Mr. Harrier, who assumed that the Town Clerk was well paid, and had plenty of spare income. Mr. Riddout became so fed up with the man's persistence that he finally told his secretary that if he came to hound Mr. Riddout in his office again, he was to be told that Mr. Riddout was out.

Shortly after giving this instruction, Mr. Riddout heard, through the communicating door, which was partly open, the salesman asking the secretary if he could see the Town Clerk for a few moments. He heard his secretary say that he was out, and Mr. Harrier left the secretary's office. But when footsteps stopped outside his office door, Mr. Riddout was intrigued, and wondered what was afoot. Slowly he levered himself out of his chair, and tiptoed across his office to peer through the keyhole. He saw an eye looking back at him. Mr. Harrier got the message, and his hounding ceased.

Military discipline

Five minutes from the center of Nairobi there is an airfield. Called Wilson Airport or Nairobi West Airport, it now handles mainly light aircraft flights to National Parks and other holiday resort destinations. It has had a checkered career and, during WW II, was a Fleet Air Arm (Naval Air Force) base - over 300 miles from the coast. Most of the aircraft stationed there at that time were Seafires, the Naval equivalent of the famous Spitfire.

There were a number of rather languid officers around Nairobi, referred to as the NNN Brigade (Never North of Nairobi), who were extremely competent in keeping themselves well away from 'the sharp end'. They managed to avoid the war in Abyssinia, the North African Campaign, the battle for Madagascar, and later, the Burma Campaign. But they did manage to acquire the appropriate campaign medals and promotions.

One NNN officer was the second-in-command of the naval air force base at Nairobi West. We'll know him by the name of Claude Watson-Watt. He held a senior rank and had a chest covered with campaign medals. He was one of those that today might be said to 'kick ass'.

One Monday W-W arrived at Nairobi West nursing a hangover. He felt the need to harass someone. An opportunity presented itself immediately. A junior officer failed to salute him.

"Hey you!" he yelled. The junior officer took no notice and walked on.

"Hey you!" shouted W-W again. The young officer halted and turned to face a furious senior officer.

"Hello. Are you speaking to me?"

"Are you speaking to me WHAT?" bawled W-W.

"No, old boy. I never said a word," said the young man innocently.

W-W turned a dangerous puce color. This wasn't going according to plan. He gathered himself.

"Come to my office immediately," he gritted.

On reaching the office, W-W sat down, and the offender looked around for another chair. He was an amiable young man and he thought W-W wanted a chat but, before he could sit down, W-W screamed at him.

"One: You failed to salute me. Two: When you speak to a senior officer you call him SIR. Three: You do not call me old boy. Do you understand?"

"Oh yes! But I didn't see you," blurted the junior officer.

"I didn't see you WHAT?" screamed W-W.

"Well there you are, then. I didn't see you and you didn't see me." The young officer was now thoroughly confused.

"SIR! " exploded W-W.

It dawned on the junior officer that he was supposed to address the furious senior officer as Sir, and from then on things began to sort themselves out. W-W clearly didn't believe that the young man hadn't seen him, so he refused to accept this excuse for his failure to salute. Although the young man apologized profusely, and now shouted "SIR" after each sentence, W-W was not mollified.

"Get your disgusting self out there onto the parade ground, and march smartly back and forth. When you reach the far end, smartly salute the flag. Perform a smart about-turn, and march smartly to the other end. There you halt, carry out a smart about-turn and march smartly back to the flag. There you will halt, salute the flag and carry out a smart about-turn, and you will go on doing that until I order you to stop. DO YOU UNDERSTAND?"

"Yes - SIR!"

"Well carry on then. Get yourself out there!" shouted W-W.

The young officer hurried to carry out his orders - smartly.

W-W leaned back in his chair and began to relax. He put his feet up on his desk, and watched the junior officer marching back and forth, saluting the flag. He sighed deeply with satisfaction. The Commanding Officer arrived. W-W heard his superior officer in his office next door. After a minute or so, the CO came in to W-W's office.

"Oh. Hello old boy," greeted W-W. "Decent weekend?" He leaned comfortably back in his chair, and locked his hands behind his head. "Had a hell of a party myself. Good old Muthaiga Country Club! Boy, have I got a head!"

The Commanding Officer (CO) turned to look out of the window to see at what W-W was gazing.

"What's that young fool doing out there?" he asked.

W-W explained.

"Damned glad to learn somebody here is insisting on a bit of discipline. Things have become too lax. Good show!" The CO frowned. "One thing worries me. He's not saluting anything at this end. Tell you what," he continued. "You go out and take his salute at this end, then march smartly to the flag, halt, about turn and take his salute at that end too. Then march smartly back to this end, halt, about turn and take his salute again. And go on doing that until I order you to stop. And, in future, get your bloody feet off that desk, and stand up when I come into your office. And address me as SIR, not old boy. Now get out there and let's see you performing smartly for a change!"

"YES, SIR! " shouted W-W smartly.

11

Solus

The headboy at Kenton, Ken Stanning, or Solus as he was known to his peers, believed that small boys needed to be regularly disciplined. He was about fourteen and a fine athlete. I was about ten, an exceptionally fast runner and excessively self-opinionated. The Scouts and the Cubs played a game in which the Scouts put their hats at one end of a field and the Cubs put theirs at the other. A track divided the field, and each side defended their half. The aim was to race past all members of the opposing team and grab a hat. On being tagged by a member of the opposing team, you became a prisoner, and could only be released by a member of your team getting through. He could either release a prisoner or take a hat, and walk back to his side of the field, with hat or released prisoner, without being tagged.

The Scouts were handicapped by having to try to collect twenty hats while the cubs had only ten to collect. In this way the advantage of size that the Scouts had was reduced, and the playing field was leveled. The Cubs won the first game which only added to Solus's rage.

In the second game my job was to cover Stanning. I, as a junior, was supposed to call him by his last name. He stood on one side of the track, and I stood opposite him.

"If you try to cross the track, I'll tag you, Solus." I said insolently.

"What did you call me?" Solus's eyes blazed.

"You heard," I answered cheekily. I wasn't learning. Although we were playing a game, I wasn't permitted to address him other than by his last name.

"Report to me in the dormitory tonight," he snapped.

I did, and was beaten on my pajama covered posterior four times with a metal buckled Scout belt for being insolent. I clenched my teeth in rage but said nothing. I tried not to show the pain I was suffering, and walked to my bed with my head held high. I gained the sympathy and admiration of my pals.

The school, for the duration of the war, had moved to a hotel. The school's own buildings had been commandeered by the armed forces as a military hospital. The large room we used as a dormitory had been a dance hall. The wooden floor was smooth, and ideal for skating in leather soled slippers. Naturally, this activity was banned.

One evening shortly after Solus had beaten me, I was walking down the dormitory to my bed, when I remembered that I wanted to tell something to one of my friends. I was, at that moment, passing his bed. I braked abruptly and, in doing so, slid a foot or so.

"Come here," yelled Solus from his bed at the end of the dormitory. "I saw you skating. Go and report to Mr. Taylor, and tell him why I've sent you."

Mr. Taylor, whom I didn't like, had his rooms next to the dormitory. I explained my visit, and was questioned tersely.

"Go into my bedroom, and get my cane from beside the wardrobe and a pillow from my bed." I sighed knowing

104

that my posterior was certain to suffer yet again. I returned with the cane and pillow.

"Give me the cane and fold the pillow over that chair," instructed Mr. Taylor.

I did as I was bid, thinking that I was to bend over the chair, and that the pillow was to support my tummy. I was puzzled because, normally, I would have expected to be told just to bend over. The chair was a new element in the ritual of corporal punishment. But why make it comfortable with a pillow?

"Stand back," ordered Mr. Taylor. I did so, and Mr. Taylor gave the pillow six hard whacks with his cane.

You swine, I thought. You are just demonstrating how hard you're going to beat me.

"Put these back where you found them." Mr. Taylor handed me his cane and the pillow.

I was now totally confused. When I returned from his bedroom, Mr. Taylor said, "Now go back to the dormitory. I suggest you rub your behind. Pretend you have just had six of the best. Never say a word about what has just happened, to anyone."

I did as I was bid. I think Mr. Taylor had heard Solus had beaten me with a Scout belt a few days earlier, and thought the punishment unjust. So, I got away without being caned, but couldn't brag about it as I'd been told to keep mum. I couldn't resist letting Solus know just before the end of term. This irked him, but it was too late for him to take the retribution he threatened. Solus left Kenton to go on to high school. I thought I'd never see him again.

But Solus was to attend the Prince of Wales School (PoW), and I was to follow him there four years later. By that time he had finished schooling, and had been appointed temporary Physical Training Instructor.

His idea of PT was like that of the instructors in U.S. Army boot camps: Driving victims to the limits of their endurance. Each boy had to demonstrate how many pushups and pull-ups he could do. This we did with enthusiasm, as they were sort of macho tests. The result was noted in Solus's little black book and, in the event of a boy failing to carry out some exercise to Solus's satisfaction, he was told to do as many pushups as he was capable of, as recorded in the little black book.

I had been ill during the school vacation with a very serious case of measles, and had not recovered my full fitness. Towards the end of a hard PT session, we were instructed to hang on the wall bars, and raise our legs horizontally before us.

One boy, John (Granny) Eames, was just not designed for such exercises, so Solus went over to help him get his legs horizontal, in the hope that Granny would be able to hold them in that position for a second or two, so that Solus could see the whole class in the correct position.

Meanwhile, the rest of us had been holding the position for about half a minute, as best we could. My hands were sweating after nearly 45 minutes of hard going, and my grip on the top wall bar slipped.

I got down, wiped my hands on my shorts, and was getting back into position when Solus turned round and saw me. Quick reference to his little black book elicited the information that I could do fifty pushups. So that is what I now had to do.

I barely managed, and virtually collapsed at the end, which was also the end of the session. Friends helped me to the changing room where, after some minutes, I felt better.

As I left the gym, my arch-enemy was standing by the door smirking, and I muttered that one day I'd get him. Half an hour later I had to be helped from class to the dispensary, temporarily blind and vomiting. I couldn't enunciate properly and was clearly in distress.

My mother was phoned, and she collected me, took me home, and called the doctor. He examined me, and listened to my heart with his stethoscope. He finally announced that I had strained my heart, which had actually moved sideways in my chest. I was confined to bed, and my father went to see the Headmaster of the school. This resulted in Solus's dismissal. He left to become a farmer, and I never saw him again.

But all that is in the future and we must return to the period when I was at Kenton College.

12

Public = Privately Owned.   Government = Publicly Owned

Kenton College, a public school (privately owned), took boys from about the age of seven to about thirteen. The curriculum was designed to prepare the boys to sit an examination for entry into English public schools.

Before the outbreak of WW II, most white Kenya residents were British and had close relatives in Britain. Children from Kenya attending school in Britain spent vacations with their relatives, and every 4 years or so, their parents would take six months 'Home leave', when they would be able to participate in the job of rearing their off-spring.

The government run schools (publicly owned) in Kenya were considered third rate, suitable only for the progeny of the less affluent Europeans and 'officials' - government expatriate employees. The reputation was probably unfair, although it is possibly true to say that the best government school teachers went to schools for Africans, as the pupils were far keener to receive education, and absorbed learning like sponges. The offspring of white settlers were considered idle, recalcitrant, and had brains into which it was most difficult to drum academic knowledge.

They were more interested in hunting, shooting, fishing and, dare I say it, girls, and of course their brains had been addled by the sun.

Kenton College was a grammar school. This means that we were taught Latin. We pupils could see no useful purpose in trying to learn a long dead language, besides which, John Taylor, the Latin teacher was unpopular. He was humorless and sarcastic. He also coached us in cricket but, unless one was naturally gifted, he ignored even the keenest attempts to improve. Somehow he did manage to pound some Latin into my addled brain.

We also had to learn French, another seemingly futile exercise. French was the language of the diplomats but I cannot think of a single boy who was attracted to that occupation which we considered one for smarmy fops. Somehow, our teacher did manage to pound some French into my addled brain.

I was not the only student who thought that the Kiswahili language should be taught as, at that time - and until several years after independence, it was widely used between the tribes and races in East Africa. At Kenton we were not allowed to speak Kiswahili. After Kenya gained independence, Kiswahili was designated as the National Language and English as the Official Language. Some African Members tried to use Kiswahili in Parliament, but found their own command of the language inadequate, the fluency of other Members indifferent, and the scope of Kiswahili deficient in scientific and technical terms.

An Indifferent Scholar at Kenton

Kenton College was a good private school but, like most schools in Kenya, many of the teachers had been called up for war service, and we were left with those who were too old for the military or were disabled. Those unfortunates who remained to try to instill education into us, a reluctant rabble, formed a hard core of professional, trained and experienced teachers. Some of those who were engaged to take the place of those who had gone to war, were unable to control the boys so, though they knew their subject, they were not able to teach it.

Although I enjoyed school life, and said so at the time, I was not a good scholar. Nearly all my school reports said 'could do better' and this was certainly true. I was too easily diverted from studying, and I think that this was due, in part, to my having attended four schools before going to Kenton at the age of eight. Clearly I had missed elements of some subjects, and blank patches led to difficulties in understanding or gaining competency, due to embarrassment and my being too shy to ask for further enlightenment

Two things helped me with my left-handed writing problem. First, when I was about nine, 'relief' nibs became available. Why they were called 'relief' nibs I do not know, but they surely afforded me some relief They were made of malleable brass, and had a squared tip which could be bent backwards a few degrees so that it didn't jab into the paper.

It wasn't possible to write with thick down strokes and thin upward strokes, which was the preferred style, but writing was easier. The problem of smearing what I'd just written remained, but I learned to use blotting paper under my hand to prevent the worst smudging.

An obstacle that remained was that every teacher tried to make me write with my right hand, and this problem wasn't solved until I heard that King George VI stuttered due to his having been made to try to be right handed.

Within seconds of my hearing this, I s-s-started a t-t-terrible s-s-stutter and after a f-f-few d-d-days I was t-t-told t-t-to write l-l-left handed if I wanted to. Thanks to the impatience of the teacher, my stutter was miraculously cured. My writing was still abominable, but I was a happier little boy.

The school had a library, stocked mainly with popular books for boys, and I began to read a lot. My introduction to reading for pleasure occurred quite suddenly when I was about nine. I'd picked up a book belonging to my sister Elizabeth during a school vacation, and read it. I found the adventures of a girl and her horse on a ranch in Kenya thrilling.

At school, weekends sometimes dragged, and there was plenty of time to read. Sometimes I read a whole book on a Sunday, if it was a good adventure story. I didn't read 'serious' literature of the sort that we were required to read for school work.

Mum, a voracious reader, had been a librarian, and was delighted that she and her, until now, feckless son were to share enjoyment in reading. Mum began to think I was not such a bad lad. A close friendship started to develop.

A Gentleman's Club?

Although reading, sports and hobbies created diversions from boredom, we did get into silly pastimes at Kenton, and a few of us formed The Wuzzy Club. I suppose this never had a membership of more than seven, and consisted of five or six hard-core ten-year-olds, who swore to come to one another's aid all through life. We dragged on cigarettes made from semi-dried rose petals, rolled in brown paper. We smoked in a young mango tree, the branches and leaves of which formed a dense cover which hid us from sight. The hide was in direct line-of-sight from the Masters' Common Room, but was too far away for the masters to see smoke issuing in clouds from the tree.

I got into trouble with Wuzzie Club members when one of the larger branches of our hide began to sag, making a window which would allow the masters to see into the leafy canopy. It was decided to tie the sagging branch to the one above, and I was selected to rest the sagging branch on my shoulder, reach up to grasp the branch above and heave to raise the sagging branch to its original position.

III

I was aware of the brittleness of mango trees, and told my four Wuzzy Club co-members that the branch might break. They jeered at me saying that, just because my Dad was in the timber industry, it didn't mean that I knew anything about trees. So, I did as I was bid. The branch broke. There was a chorus of acrimony.

"Oh, Gill you clumsy idiot."

"Oh, Gill you silly fool".

"You did that on purpose, you donkey."

"Yeah, you did that deliberately."

"Grab the bugger."

I was seized by my fellow Wuzzies, and found guilty of deliberately breaking the branch, thus making the tree useless as a hide. Dragged to a netball court and, with my chest against the corner of a goal post and two Wuzzy Club members on each arm, I was helpless.

"When I yell jerk, we all yank as hard as we can together," instructed the Wuzzy Club captain, Jeremy.

"Hang on. Let me get a good grip," said Robin through clenched teeth.

"Ready?" asked Jeremy. "JERK."

My shoulders were wrench out of joint.

"AAAAH," I cried in agony. A couple of my torturers blanched. Had they overdone things, they seemed to ask themselves. In an attempt to suspend hostilities, Simon patted my shoulder. My shoulders were on fire. This was bad enough, but Simon grabbed my hanging arms above the elbows and, with an upward jerk, shoved my shoulders back into joint.

"AAAAH," I repeated. Hairs on the back of my neck stood on end. My eyes watered, and I all but passed out. I staggered and it must have been apparent to the Club members that they had gone too far.

After a few minutes the pain subsided a little.

"You bastards. You'll pay for that." I gritted, and challenged each member in turn to a fight behind the tennis courts.

The end screens of the courts hid the area from the view of the Master's Common Room, and this was the place where we used to settle our differences. So, about two weeks later, one by one over a period of a few days, I took my revenge. I was a skillful boxer, and treated each torturer with quick one, two.

"AAAAH," squealed each in turn to my intense satisfaction, and covered a bloody nose, a thick ear and/or a split lip with his hand

I had no further trouble, and the Wuzzy Club members built a grass shelter, in the style of a small igloo, where we could smoke, and have the occasional feast on delicacies smuggled back to school after the half-term day off. Canned sardines, peaches, pears and corned beef, all mixed up with bits of dried grass and dirt, were considered a real treat.

After we left Kenton I lost contact with the other Wuzzy members. One joined the police, and caught me one evening driving a car-load of friends the wrong way around a road divider at a junction. We were late for a movie, and I had taken a short cut right in front of an unlit police car in which my chum from Wuzzie days was sitting with several constables, waiting for some idiot to break the rules of the road. He let me off, radioing back to headquarters that I had eluded him. So he lived up to the oath we had sworn years ago at school. Somehow his parents managed to get him to England during WW II for his secondary school education at Marlborough, one of the five most famous English public schools. He returned to Kenya with a polish, refinement and dignity that we barbarians, who attended the Prince of Wales School, never achieved. But he did abandon his wife and family to run off with a rich New York socialite. So maybe his education was not as good as his parents had paid for, lacking the morals that a public school education was supposed to impart.

13

Artful boxing

At Kenton I found that my boxing skills, learned at Muthaiga School, hadn't left me. I was in the same situation in that I could beat everybody but one, who was very much better than I. Simon (Sim) Wollen was about my size, weight and age, and besides being good at sports he was also a good student. He had been a Wuzzy Club member, and I had managed to beat him in a bare fisted fight, he being a better boxer than I, but not as good a fighter. Sim was to become an attorney and a rather serious member of society.

At Kenton, as at Muthaiga School, we had a very good boxing coach, an aging ex-Royal Air Force Featherweight Champion. The sport was supervised by Mr. Cramb, the Headmaster who had also been a good boxer in his youth. The sport is one in which the contenders spar with the aim of making clean contact with the opponent. Hard hitting was frowned upon. One is supposed to avoid being struck by defending oneself with gloves, arms and by footwork, dodging and weaving.

Properly taught, the sport is a good one, imparting confidence by teaching self-defense, temper control, and agility. It is gratifying, so long as you don't get hurt. The gloves prevent serious injury. Today head-guards further reduce the possibility of head injury. I gave up the sport at the PoW at about the age of fourteen because we had no instructor. Occasionally fights broke out in which no gloves were used and, from boxing experience, I was able to hand out fairly serious pain without getting hurt myself. I could land heavy punches to body and shoulders, but avoided head shots as these were likely to cause injury to my hands.

During a holiday by the sea, I was a guest of friends who owned the holiday beach house, a bare fisted fight erupted between another guest and me. I had gone to the outside privy and was contemplating the ways of the world when a pebble flew through the unglazed window above the door.

"Ouch," I yelled as a pebble hit me on the head. My startled cry was greeted by giggles, and another pebble was thrown in through the fanlight. From his guffaws, I could tell it was Peter Upson.

"Cut it out, you bugger," I cried with rage rising.

My objections in the strongest terms were met by a stone hurtling at my head. Luckily, I was able to deflect the missile with my arm, and I became furious. Peter shouted that he was only trying to hurry me.

I emerged from the privy to find Peter outside with an inane smirk on his face. I walked away, but stopped when I heard Peter close the door. I quietly moved back towards the privy, and I allowed him a few moments to settle down, before lobbing a handful of pebbles in through the window. Now it was Peter's turn to yell protests, and my turn to chuckle.

"You bloody swine," he yelled.

Another handful of pebbles and Peter burst out like an enraged bull. Emulating a toreador, I stepped nimbly to one side, and lashed out with my left fist at his shoulder. He ducked and caught the blow on the side of his head. That took the fight out of him. He never learned that I'd broken my hand.

The following day, I saved him from drowning. He got into trouble in the spring tide waves and panicked. I had to punch him to bring him to his senses or we would both have drowned. I hit him with my right fist while holding him with my injured hand, which caused intense pain. The wretch never bothered to thank me for saving his worthless life.

An eerie experience.

The only time I really avoided a fight was on a strange occasion. I was about 11 years old, and one afternoon was sitting at my desk during the prep period - short for preparation-work to be done after normal school hours ready for the next day. The sun shone across my desk through the open door. I looked at my watch and noted that the time was exactly 3 p.m.

A shadow fell across my desk and I looked up to see Michael Frisby standing in the doorway, sharpening his pencil with the long blade of a pocket knife. Michael was a disturbed boy whose father had died. His mother had remarried and his stepfather disliked Michael. After his mother died, his stepfather frequently beat the boy. Then his stepfather remarried a much younger woman. She was very attractive, and in an attempt, perhaps, to show Michael sympathy, took him to bed and introduced him to sex and eroticism. This I learned when Michael and I became good friends, and he used me as a confidant.

Michael was an exceptionally big, strong boy, but at thirteen was well behind his age group academically. He was inclined to lose his temper easily, and fought like a madman when he did so. When I saw him standing in the doorway, a feeling of deja vu came over me. The sunlight falling across my desk, the time, Michael's stance, the pencil, the knife, I

117

was so sure that it had all happened before that I was struck dumb.

Michael walked past me to his desk, and sat down to struggle with his prep. I sat and thought. The incident had seemed to have happened before, but I knew it hadn't. Then it came to me that when 'it had happened before', I'd made some cheeky remark to Michael, who had lost his temper, and struck at me, knife in hand. For the first time in my life, deja vu saved me from a potentially dangerous incident.

Michael wasn't a good boxer as he couldn't control his temper, but I was not inclined to tackle him when he had a knife in his hand.

I missed him when he was taken from school. Later, he managed to get into the Navy by lying about his age. His ship visited Mombasa, and he came up to Nairobi for a visit. He threw himself under a bus right in the center of the town in full view of hundreds of Saturday shoppers. A very sad ending for a badly confused boy.

And he's a friend?

Another friend who lived near me was Bruce Holden. He was a short, sturdy lad with good gymnastic ability. He was also a good boxer.

Bruce and I were walking to his home from my house one day when I spotted a flint ball approximately four inches in diameter. It must have been dropped there by somebody who had found it in a river as it was smooth as well as being perfectly spherical - a treasure to a boy of ten.

"Mine," I yelled, and walked forward to pick it up, but Bruce raced ahead, snatched it away and claimed it as his.

"I saw it first," I declared hotly.

"I picked it up first," Bruce claimed.

"I shouted out first. And it's closest to my home," I was adamant. And so an argument developed. I challenged him to a fight but he declined - which was sensible as I had a much longer reach - so I called him a coward, and said he could keep the thing. But I was not satisfied.

A few days later, Bruce and I went to the swimming pool. I'd not been with him there before. We took separate changing booths, and when I came out I found Bruce standing on the edge of the pool. I crept up, and pushed him in. He sank to the bottom, and came up thrashing his arms about in a panic. I was amazed that he wasn't able to swim, and dived under him and, by walking across the bottom of the pool, carried him over my head and above the water to the pool side. He clambered out spluttering.

"I can't breath under water," he blubbered.

After he had recovered, I offered to teach him how to swim if he would give back my stone. So, a deal was struck. Bruce learned the rudiments of swimming, and I recovered the treasured flint ball, which I dropped when walking home. I was left with two half spheres which I threw away in disgust.

Bruce felt he'd been hard done by, and was still angered by my calling him a coward when he had declined to fight me. After another tiff, he took a shot at me with his .22 rifle as I rode away. He used .22 'shorts' and the slug hit the frame of my bicycle before hitting my lower leg. I didn't stop, but rode home where I found that the slug had stuck flush with the surface of my flesh. I dug it out with a pocket knife quite easily, put on a sticking plaster, and said nothing. It healed well enough. I never told Bruce that his slug had hit me. That might have given him satisfaction, and the feeling that he had avenged himself. Our friendship was at an end. Shortly afterwards, he left for school in South Africa, the real home of his parents.

'Bosom' Martin and I break records

Another of my school friends was Bosom Martin. He lived a couple of hundred yards from me, and I saw quite a lot of him during the holidays. He was nicknamed Bosom after he had mispronounced the word when reading aloud a passage to the class from a school book about a mother gathering her frightened son to her bosom. He pronounced the word to rhyme with possum, which caused much mirth, and he was called Bosom thereafter.

When we were about eleven, he was given a .22 rifle for his birthday and his father taught him how to use it for target practice in the garden. He used .22 'shorts', a low powered ammunition suitable for practice shooting. Bosom had a limited number of target cards, and, when these were used up, we looked for something else to shoot at. Under a radio/gramophone table in the living room was a pile of records which, Bosom said, nobody ever listened to. So, taking them from their sleeves, which we left all over the lounge floor, we took them into the garden. The idea was to try to put the bullet through the hole in the middle from 25 yards. We weren't always successful in this endeavor, and soon there was a pile of broken records on the terraced lawn at the foot of the rockery.

Mrs. Martin had been out shopping, and Mr. Martin was at work. As the last record was shattered, Mrs. Martin entered the lounge to find the record sleeves all over the carpet. She rushed out to find her beloved son and a strange rapscallion, rifle in hand, who, in her opinion, had misled her son into smashing a valuable collection of irreplaceable classical records.

She came to where we were standing looking at the devastation we had caused. Her jaw dropped and her body stiffened. She began to shake.

"What have you done? What have you done to my records? Why have you destroyed all my lovely music? What on earth got into you?"

She swung round on me. "You...you...horrible little boy......"

Bosom stepped into the breech. "Mum, I am to blame..."

"No you are NOT. You would never do such a thing. This hooligan led you to..."

"But Mrs. Martin....." I started.

"You...you brute." Mrs Martin was quivering with rage and was finding speech difficult.

"But Mrs..."

"Don't lie to me boy."

"But..."

"What will your parents say?"

"Bu..."

"I don't suppose they appreciate beautiful operatic arias."

"B..."

"Go away! Go away and don't ever come here again."

I turned to Bosom, gave him a little conspiratorial grin, shrugged and ran homewards. I was resentful. I had not been allowed to explain, and Bosom's confession had been brushed aside. What my explanation would have been, I had no idea. I hadn't wanted to snitch on my friend. Anyway, I consoled myself with the thought that I'd see my pal at school. I was never allowed to visit Bosom at his home again. The Martins moved to another house a long way from our house. Bosom remained one of my friends at school but we never discussed the day we broke all records.

Meanwhile, Mum, my Aunt Norah, my two sisters and I were to go to the coast for a two week holiday. As I trotted home, I pushed aside all feelings of guilt. Well, who liked Caruso anyway? I eagerly looked forward to adventures by the sea although I could never have foreseen what those adventures would be. Explosions, cattle stampedes, love affairs, buried treasure.....

Additional Reading

Markham, Beryl: nee Clutterbuck. See autobiography, *'West With the Night'*;

'Beryl Markham', biography by Errol Trzebinski;

'Beryl', by Aimee Lamb - **Summary:** Taken to East Africa at four, Beryl grew up playing and hunting with local tribesmen, killing a wild boar and being mauled by a lion by age nine. At eighteen she was left by her destitute father with her horse, saddlebags and wits. She turned to horse training and was acclaimed the best horse trainer six times. By twenty-eight she was flying mail and medicine and conducting safaris to uncharted areas. She was confidante/love of the Duke of Gloucester and Denys Finch Hatton. The first to fly solo across the Atlantic in 1936 she was feted and paraded in New York. Her book "West with the Night" was acclaimed by Hemingway who said "that I was ashamed of myself as a writer." - Aimee Lamb

'White Mischief', by James Fox. The Happy Valley crowd of which Beryl Markham was on the fringe. A small group of high living, degenerate expatriate British aristocracy, some of whom were the 'black sheep' of their families. Their families in Britain, eager to rid themselves of delinquent members, provided them with incomes on the understanding that they would leave the UK to live overseas. They were termed 'Remittance Men' and, in Kenya, tended to keep themselves apart from the serious minded, hard working settlers, who scorned them as idlers, and wastrels.

GLOSSARY

Box Body Car. The 1927 basic 'box body' car was completed in Kenya by local auto body builders, using wood, angle iron and canvas. Cars were imported with chassis, engines, transmissions, and all the suspension, steering and body work as far as the front bench seat, fixed to the chassis and with steel running boards and fenders over front and rear wheels. This was all mounted on wheels fitted with the skinny tires of the day. The locally made body consisted of a wooden box, as the name indicates, built onto the chassis behind the seat, within the rear fenders, with a roof mounted on vertical angle irons and to the windshield frame extending back over the box. Onto both sides of the box were two additional boxes extending over the rear fenders. These had hinged lids, which served as lockable boxes for tools, digging implements, chains and a few spare parts. There were no doors for the driver and passenger, but the body was cut away to allow ease of access. Attached all round the roof were canvas curtains, normally kept rolled up, to provide protection against rain when unrolled and fastened down onto turn-buckles fitted to the body.

Brit de-tribalized. One who has no British regional accent and cannot therefore be pigeon holed in the social scale by the Brits, who then deem one to be some sort of alien.

Kanga. A cotton cloth about 5 ft by 3 ft worn by women who wrap the cloth around their bodies under their arms.

Kanzu. A long-sleeved gown reaching from neck to ankles, usually plain white or yellowish brown. It was found by European employers to be a sensible garment for house servants as it was inexpensive and generally 'one size fits all', although much hated by the servants. Usually worn with a red embroidered cummerbund and sleeveless close fitting jacket.

Kikoi. A cotton cloth about 5 ft by 3 ft worn by men around their waists like a sarong.

Muthaiga Country Club. A popular meeting place for settlers four miles to the north of the center of Nairobi. It offered comfortable accommodation, an excellent menu and a well stocked bar. Members could enjoy tennis, squash (racket ball), a swimming pool and a library. It became associated with the Happy Valley set, who used it as a venue when they came to Nairobi. Because of this, the Club had a slightly nefarious reputation and some settlers shunned it. Dad refused to become a member but, soon after his death, Mum eagerly joined the Club - purely for the good meals and library, so she insisted.

Panga. A machete-like implement widely used with considerable skill throughout East Africa to cut bushes, trees, reeds, grass and meat. It is also used to dig and as a weapon. About 22 in. long including a 5 in. wooden handle, the thickness of the spring steel blade tapers from 1/8 to 1/16 of an inch. The width increases from 1 ¾ in. below the handle to about 3 in. toward the end of the blade which either tapers to a point or ends with a wide broad curve. The latter type is favored to dig post holes. The handle comprises of two pieces of shaped hardwood riveted to each side of the steel blade. The implement is well balanced and is kept sharp.

Swahili. (Properly Kiswahili). The *lingua franca* of East Africa. The language developed over several hundred years when Arab slavers dominated the area. There is no Swahili tribe. A *Mswahili* is a *Kiswahili* speaking person. *Waswahili* are *Kiswahili* speaking people. The language has origins in the languages of the coastal tribes of East Africa and Zanzibar, Arabic, Persian and Turkish. It has also borrowed from English, Hindi, German and there are traces of Portuguese. Arab slavers from Oman, Egypt, Saudi Arabia, Persia, Jordan and Syria operated, in safety, from the islands of Zanzibar and Pemba off the coast of Tanzania.

Kiswahili has five vowels each of which has only one sound:

A as in c<u>a</u>r; *E* as in g<u>e</u>t; *I* as ee in kn<u>ee</u>; *O* as in f<u>or</u>; *U* as oo in b<u>oo</u>k. Diphthongs of two vowels are pronounced by running the two vowel sounds together as in the following examples: *Nairobi; shauri; tao,; toa;*

Ch as in chicken. *Th* as in thick. *Dh* as th in there.

The penultimate syllable is always stressed. Kiswahili words employ suffixes and this alters the pronunciation:

M<u>e</u>sa - table. *Mes<u>a</u>ni* - on the table. *Ch<u>u</u>mba* - room. *Chumb<u>a</u>ni* - in the room.

Words borrowed from Arabic, English and other languages do not use suffixes:

Ndani ya motoka - in the motor car (NOT *motokani*)

To simplify I have omitted the prefixes *M* and *Wa* in front of the names of tribes: *Kikuyu* instead of *Mkikuyu* - a Kikuyu person or *Wakikuyu* - Kikuyu people.

About the Author

Born in Kenya, East Africa, of English parents in December 1930, Len lived there until 1989. During his childhood, among his family and African servants, he ignored the dismay he caused them.

He enjoyed life. Even a period at boarding school offered Len scope for devilment. His absence at school relieved those at home of the complications that always seemed to attend his presence. His school teachers and friends had to bear the burden.

By the development of youthful arrogance, and in blissful ignorance of the vexations he caused, he was unaware of the necessity to balance humor with seriousness.

Africans dubbed him with the nickname *Mpenda raha* (he who enjoys a good time). Len insists that a shot-glass of humor helps the worries go down.

The inspiration in his life, Kaye, recognised Len's flair for storytelling, and insisted that, having reached three score years and ten, he get down to writing his memoirs.

Len now lives in Glenwood Springs, Colorado with his wife, Kaye and Shih-tzu, Bandit.

ISBN 1553951070-7

9 781553 951070